John Cotton Dana

A Library Primer

John Cotton Dana

A Library Primer

ISBN/EAN: 9783337312022

Printed in Europe, USA, Canada, Australia, Japan

Cover: Foto ©Thomas Meinert / pixelio.de

More available books at **www.hansebooks.com**

A Library Primer

John Cotton Dana

Library Bureau, Chicago

1899

Copyright, 1899,
by
Library Bureau

To
Samuel S. Green, William I. Fletcher,
and Charles A. Cutter

PREFACE.

A library primer was published in the first six numbers of Public Libraries in 1896. It was quite largely made up of extracts from an article by Dr W. F. Poole on The organization and management of public libraries, which formed part of the report on Public libraries in the U. S., published by the U. S. Bureau of education in 1876; from W. I. Fletcher's Public libraries in America; from Mary W. Plummer's Hints to small libraries; and from papers in the Library journal and A. L. A. proceedings.

At the request of a number of people interested I have revised, rewritten, and extended the original draft for publication in book form. Additional material has been taken from many sources. I have tried to give credit in good measure. The prevailing tendency among librarians is to share ideas, to give to one another the benefit of all their suggestions and experiences. The result is a large fund of library knowledge which is common property. From this fund most of this book is taken.

The Library Primer is what its name implies. It does not try to be exhaustive in any part of the field. It tries to open up the subject of library management for the small library, and to show how large it is and how much librarians have yet to learn and to do.

The City library, J. C. D.
Springfield, Mass.

CONTENTS

CHAPTER		PAGE
I,	The beginnings—Library law	9
II,	Preliminary work	10
III,	What does a public library do for a community?	12
IV,	General policy of the library	15
V,	Trustees	17
VI,	The librarian	20
VII,	The trained librarian	23
VIII,	Rooms, building, fixtures, furniture	25
IX,	Things needed in beginning work	30
X,	The Library Bureau	35
XI,	Selecting books	39
XII,	Reference books for a small library	46
XIII,	Reference work	53
XIV,	Reading room	57
XV,	List of periodicals	61
XVI,	Buying books	63
XVII,	Ink and handwriting	69
XVIII,	Care of books	73
XIX,	Accessioning	76
XX,	Classifying	78
XXI,	Decimal classification	81
XXII,	Expansive classification	84
XXIII,	Author numbers or book marks	91
XXIV,	Shelf list	92
XXV,	Cataloging	94
XXVI,	Preparing books for the shelf	99
XXVII,	Binding and mending	103

CONTENTS

XXVIII,	Pamphlets	108
XXIX,	Public documents	110
XXX,	Checking the library	113
XXXI,	Lists, bulletins, and printed catalogs	114
XXXII,	Charging systems	116
XXXIII,	Meeting the public	122
XXXIV,	The public library for the public	123
XXXV,	Advice to a librarian	126
XXXVI,	The librarian as a host	128
XXXVII,	Making friends for the library	131
XXXVIII,	Public libraries and recreation	133
XXXIX,	Books as useful tools	134
XL,	Village library successfully managed	135
XLI,	Rules for the public	137
XLII,	Rules for trustees and employés	140
XLIII,	Reports	146
XLIV,	Library legislation	147
XLV,	A. L. A. and other library associations	152
XLVI,	Library schools and classes	154
XLVII,	Library department of N. E. A	156
XLVIII,	Young people and the schools	157
XLIX,	How can the library assist the school?	160
L,	Children's room	163
LI,	Schoolroom libraries	164
LII,	Children's home libraries	166
LIII,	Literary clubs and libraries	168
LIV,	Museums, lectures, etc	170
LV,	Rules for the care of photographs	171

Library Primer

CHAPTER I

The beginnings—Library law

If the establishment of a free public library in your town is under consideration, the first question is probably this: Is there a statute which authorizes a tax for the support of a public library? Your state library commission, if you have one, will tell you if your state gives aid to local public libraries. It will also tell you about your library law. If you have no library commission, consult a lawyer and get from him a careful statement of what can be done under present statutory regulations. If your state has no library law, or none which seems appropriate in your community, it may be necessary to suspend all work, save the fostering of a sentiment favorable to a library, until a good law is secured.

In chapters 44 and 45 will be found a list of state library commissions, important provisions in library laws, and the names of the states having the best library laws at present.

Before taking any definite steps, learn about the beginnings of other libraries by writing to people who have had experience, and especially to libraries in communities similar in size and character to your own. Write to some of the new libraries in other towns and villages of your state, and learn how they began. Visit several such libraries, if possible, the smaller the better if you are starting on a small scale.

CHAPTER II

Preliminary work

Often it is not well to lay great plans and invoke state aid at the very outset. Make a beginning, even though it be small, is a good general rule. This beginning, however petty it seems, will give a center for further effort, and will furnish practical illustrations for the arguments one may wish to use in trying to interest people in the movement.

Each community has different needs, and begins its library under different conditions. Consider, then, whether you need most a library devoted chiefly to the work of helping the schools, or one to be used mainly for reference, or one that shall run largely to periodicals and be not much more than a reading room, or one particularly attractive to girls and women, or one that shall not be much more than a cheerful resting-place, attractive enough to draw man and boy from street corner and saloon. Decide this question early, that all effort may be concentrated to one end, and that your young institution may suit the community in which it is to grow, and from which it is to gain its strength.

Having decided to have a library, keep the movement well before the public. The necessity of the library, its great value to the community, should be urged by the local press, from the platform, and in personal talk. Include in your canvass all citizens, irrespective of creed, business, or politics; whether educated or illiterate. Enlist the support of teachers, and through them interest children and parents. Literary, art, social, and scientific societies, Chautauqua circles, local clubs of all kinds should be champions of the movement.

In getting notices of the library's work in the newspapers, or in securing mention of it from the lecture platform, or in clubs, and literary, artistic, and musical societies, it is better to refrain from figures and to deal chiefly in general statements about what the library aims to do and what it has done.

CHAPTER III

What does a public library do for a community?

And what good does a public library do? What is it for?

1) It supplies the public with recreative reading. To the masses of the people—hard-worked and living humdrum lives—the novel comes as an open door to an ideal life, in the enjoyment of which one may forget, for a time, the hardships or the tedium of the real. One of the best functions of the public library is to raise this recreative reading of the community to higher and higher levels; to replace trash with literature of a better order.

2) A proper and worthy aim of the public library is the supplying of books on every profession, art, or handicraft, that workers in every department who care to study may perfect themselves in their work.

3) The public library helps in social and political education—in the training of citizens. It is, of course, well supplied with books and periodicals which give the thought of the best writers on the economic and social questions now under earnest discussion.

4) The highest and best influence of the library may be summed up in the single word, culture. No other word so well describes the influence of the diffusion of good reading among the people in giving tone and character to their intellectual life.

5) The free reading room connected with most of our public libraries, and the library proper as well, if it

be rightly conducted, is a powerful agent for counteracting the attractions of saloons and low resorts. Especially useful is it to those boys and young men who have a dormant fondness for reading and culture, but lack home and school opportunities.

6) The library is the ever-ready helper of the school-teacher. It aids the work of reading circles and other home-culture organizations, by furnishing books required and giving hints as to their value and use; it adds to the usefulness of courses of lectures by furnishing lists of books on the subjects to be treated; it allies itself with university extension work; in fact, the extension lecture given in connection with the free use of a good library seems to be the ideal university of the people.

The public library, then, is a means for elevating and refining the taste, for giving greater efficiency to every worker, for diffusing sound principles of social and political action, and for furnishing intellectual culture to all.

The library of the immediate future for the American people is unquestionably the free public library, brought under municipal ownership, and, to some extent, municipal control, and treated as part of the educational system of the state. The sense of ownership in it makes the average man accept and use the opportunities of the free public library while he will turn aside from book privileges in any other guise.

That the public library is a part of the educational system should never be lost sight of in the work of establishing it, or in its management. To the great mass of the people it comes as their first and only educational opportunity. The largest part of every man's education is that which he gives himself. It is for this individual, self-administered education that the public library furnishes the opportunity and the means. The schools start education in childhood; libraries carry it on.

CHAPTER IV

Suggestions as to general policy of the library

In general, remember always 1) that the public owns its public library, and 2) that no useless lumber is more useless than unused books. People will use a library, not because, in others' opinions, they ought to, but because they like to. See to it, then, that the new library is such as its owner, the public, likes; and the only test of this liking is use. Open wide the doors. Let regulations be few and never obtrusive. Trust American genius for self-control. Remember the deference for the rights of others with which you and your fellows conduct yourselves in your own homes, at public tables, at general gatherings. Give the people at least such liberty with their own collection of books as the bookseller gives them with his. Let the shelves be open, and the public admitted to them, and let the open shelves strike the keynote of the whole administration. The whole library should be permeated with a cheerful and accommodating atmosphere. Lay this down as the first rule of library management; and for the second, let it be said that librarian and assistants are to treat boy and girl, man and woman, ignorant and learned, courteous and rude, with uniform good-temper without condescension; never pertly.

Finally, bear in mind these two doctrines, tempering the one with the other: 1) that the public library is a great educational and moral power, to be wielded with a full sense of its great responsibilities, and of the corresponding danger of their neglect or perversion; 2) that the public library is not a business office, though it should be most business-like in every detail of its management; but is a center of public happiness first, of public education next.

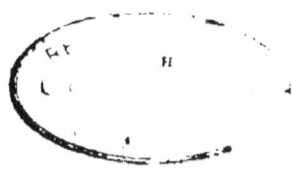

CHAPTER V
Trustees
[Condensed from paper by C. C. Soule]

1) *Size of the board.*—The library board should be small, in small towns not over three members. In cities a larger board has two advantages: it can include men exceptionally learned in library science, and it can represent more thoroughly different sections of the town and different elements in the population.

2) *Term of office.*—The board should be divided into several groups, one group going out of office each year. It would be wise if no library trustee could hold office for more than three successive terms of three years each. A library can, under this plan, keep in close touch with popular needs and new ideas.

3) *Qualifications.*—The ideal qualifications for a trustee of a public library—a fair education and love of books being taken for granted—are: sound character, good judgment, common sense, public spirit, capacity for work, literary taste, representative fitness. Don't assume that because a man has been prominent in political business or social circles he will make a good trustee. Capacity and willingness to work are more useful than a taste for literature without practical qualities. General culture and wide reading are generally more serviceable to the public library than the knowledge of the specialist or scholar. See that different sections of the town's interests are represented. Let neither politics nor religion enter into the choice of trustees.

4) *Duties.*—The trustee of the public library is elected to preserve and extend the benefits of the library as the people's university. He can learn library science only by intelligent observation and study. He should not hold his position unless he takes a lively interest in the library, attends trustees' meetings, reads the library journals, visits other libraries than his own, and keeps close watch of the tastes and requirements of his constituency. His duties include the care of funds, supervision of expenditures, determination of the library's policy, general direction of choice and purchase of books, selection of librarian and assistants, close watch of work done, and comparison of the same with results reached in other libraries.

A large board ordinarily transacts business through its chairman, secretary, treasurer, and one or more committees. It is doubtful if the librarian should act as secretary of the board. The treasurer, if he holds the funds in his hands, should always be put under bonds. It is well to have as many committees as can be actively employed in order to enlist the coöperation of all the trustees.

The executive committee should take charge of the daily work of the library, of purchases, and of the care of the building; they should carry their duties as far as possible without assuming too much of the responsibility which properly belongs to the full board. It will be best to entrust the choice of books to a book committee appointed for that purpose purely. The finance committee should make and watch investments and see that purchases are made on most favorable terms.

5) *Relations with the librarian.*—The trustees are the

responsible managers of the library; the librarian is their agent, appointed to carry out their wishes. If they have, however, a first-class librarian, the trustees ought to leave the management of the library practically to him, simply supplementing his ability without impeding it. They should leave to a librarian of good executive ability the selection, management, and dismissal of all assistants, the methods and details of library work, and the initiative in the choice of books. A wise librarian the trustees may very properly take into their confidence, and invite his presence at all meetings, where his advice would be of service.

6) *Other employés.*—Efficiency of employés can best be obtained through application of the cardinal principles of an enlightened civil service, viz., absolute exclusion of all political and personal influence, appointment for definitely ascertained fitness, promotion for merit, and retention during good behavior.

CHAPTER VI

The librarian

If circumstances permit, the librarian should be engaged even before the general character of the library and plan of administration have been determined upon. If properly selected, he or she will be a person of experience in these matters, and will be able to give valuable advice. Politics, social considerations, church sympathies, religious prejudices, family relationship—none of these should be allowed to enter into his selection. Secure an efficient officer, even at what may seem at first a disproportionate expense. Save money in other ways, but never by employing a forceless man or woman in the position of chief librarian.

Recent developments of schools of library economy, and recent rapid growth of public libraries throughout the country, have made it possible for any new library to secure good material for a librarian. If lack of funds or other conditions make it necessary to employ some local applicant, it will be wise to insist that that person, if not already conversant with library economy, shall immediately become informed on the subject. It will not be easy, it may not be possible, for trustees to inform themselves as to library organization and administration. They can, however, with very little difficulty, so far inform themselves as to be able to judge whether the person they select for their chief officer is taking pains to acquaint himself with the literature of the subject, or trying to get in touch with the knowledge and experience of others. They should not submit for a moment to ignorance or indifference on the part of their chosen administrator. Success or failure of a library, as of a business, depends on the ability of the man or woman at its head, and only trained men and women should be in charge. The business of the librarian is a profession, and a practical knowledge of the subject is never so much needed as in starting a new enterprise.

The librarian should have culture, scholarship, and executive ability. He should keep always in advance of his community, and constantly educate it to make greater demands upon him. He should be a leader and a teacher, earnest, enthusiastic, and intelligent. He should be able to win the confidence of children, and wise to lead them by easy steps from good books to the best. He has the greatest opportunity of any teacher in the community. He should be the teacher of teachers. He should make the library a school for the young, a college for adults, and the constant center of such educational activity as will make wholesome and inspiring themes the burden of the common thought. He should be enough of a bookworm to have a decided taste and fondness for books, and at the same time not enough to be such a recluse as loses sight of the point of view of those who know little of books.

As the responsible head of the institution, he should be consulted in all matters relating to its management. The most satisfactory results are obtained in those libraries where the chief librarian is permitted to appoint assistants, select books, buy supplies, make regulations, and decide methods of cataloging, classifying, and lending; all subject to the approval of the trustees. Trustees should impose responsibility, grant freedom, and exact results.

To the librarian himself one may say: Be punctual; be attentive; help develop enthusiasm in your assistants; be neat and consistent in your dress; be dignified but courteous in your manner. Be careful in your contracts; be square with your board; be concise and technical; be accurate; be courageous and self-reliant; be careful about acknowledgments; be not worshipful of your work; be careful of your health. Last of all, be yourself.

CHAPTER VII

The trained librarian in a small library

Julia A. Hopkins, of the Rochester (N. Y.) Public library, in Public Libraries, December, 1897

The value of training for the man or woman who shall take charge of a large city library is now so firmly established that no one thinks of discussing the question. If it is true that technical training is essential for the headship of a large library, why is it not equally necessary for that of a small library? Trained service is always of greater value than untrained service, be the sphere great or small. If a woman argued from the standpoint that, because the house she was to take charge of had only seven rooms instead of twenty she needed to know nothing of cooking, sweeping, and the other details of household work, I am afraid that her house and her family would suffer for her ignorance. So in many departments of library work the accident of size makes little or no difference; the work is precisely the same. The difference lies in the fact that the head of a large library oversees and directs the work done by others, where the village librarian must, in many cases, do all of the work himself. In the distinctly professional duties, such as the ordering, classifying, and cataloging of books, there is a difference only in amount between the greater and the less. And it is precisely these professional duties of which the person untrained in library work is in most cases wofully ignorant.

It is inevitable that in starting a library there should be some mistakes made; but with a trained librarian in charge, these mistakes will be fewer in number. For example, what does the novice know of classification? He realizes that the books, for convenience in use, must be grouped in classes. If he has had the use of a good library (as a college student would) he has some idea as to how the class divisions are made, and knows also that there must be some sort of notation for the classes. Necessity being the mother of invention, he contrives some plan for bringing together books on the same subject. But with the addition of books to the library and the demand which growth makes, he finds that constant changes have to be made in order to get books into their right places; and then some day he awakens to the fact that there is some perfectly well-known and adopted system of classification which will answer all his purposes, and be a great deal more satisfactory in its adaptability to the needs of his library than the one he has been struggling to evolve. Then he exclaims in despair: If I had only known of that at the beginning! He feels that the hours which he has spent in rearranging his books, taking them out of one class and putting them into another, although hours of such hard work, are in reality so many hours of wasted time. And he is right; for every minute spent in unnecessary work is so much lost time. Not only that, but it is unnecessary expense, and one of the most important things which a small library has to consider is economy.

Is it not of value to the library that its librarian should know how best to expend the money given him to use? that he should not have to regret hours of time lost over useless experiments? Surely if training teaches a librarian a wise expenditure of money and an economy of time, then training must be valuable.

CHAPTER VIII

Rooms, building, fixtures, furniture

The trustees will be wise if they appoint their librarian before they erect a building, or even select rooms, and leave these matters largely to him. They should not be in haste to build. As a rule it is better to start in temporary quarters, and let the building fund accumulate while trustees and librarian gain experience, and the needs of the library become more definite. Plans should be made with the future enlargement of the building in view; libraries increase more rapidly than is generally supposed.

Rooms of peculiar architecture are not required for the original occupation and organization of a library. The essential requirements are a central location, easy access, ample space, and sufficient light. The library and the reading room should be, if possible, on the same floor. Make the exterior attractive, and the entrance inviting. In arranging the rooms, or building, plan from the first, as already suggested, to permit visitors to go to the books themselves.

A collection of the printed matter on library architecture should be carefully studied by both trustees and librarian before any plans are made. While no specific plan can be recommended that would suit all cases, there are a few general rules that meet with the approval of the library profession as a whole. They may be thus summed up, following in the main a paper on the subject by C. C. Soule:

"A library building should be planned for library work.

Every library building should be planned especially for the kind of work to be done, and the community to be served.

The interior arrangement ought to be planned before the exterior is considered.

No convenience of arrangement should be sacrificed for mere architectural effect.

The plan should be adapted to probabilities and possibilities of growth and development.

Simplicity of decoration is essential in the working rooms and reading rooms.

The building should be planned with a view to economical administration.

The rooms for public use should be so arranged as to allow complete supervision with the fewest possible attendants.

There should be throughout as much natural light as possible.

Windows should extend up to the ceiling, to light thoroughly the upper part of every room.

Windows in a book room should be placed opposite the intervals between bookcases.

In a circulating library the books most in use should be shelved in floor cases close to the delivery desk.

A space of at least five feet should be left between floor cases. (If the public is excluded, three feet is ample.)

No shelf, in any form of bookcase, should be higher than a person of moderate height can reach without a stepladder.

Shelving for folios and quartos should be provided in every book room.

Straight flights are preferable to circular stairs.

The form of shelving which is growing in favor is the arrangement of floor cases in large rooms with space between the tops of the bookcases and the ceiling for circulation of air and the diffusion of light.

Modern library plans provide accommodations for readers near the books they want to use whatever system of shelving is adopted.

Single shelves should not be more than three feet long, on account of the tendency to sag. Ten inches between shelves, and a depth of eight inches, are good dimensions for ordinary cases. Shelves should be made movable and easily adjustable. Many devices are now in the market for this purpose, several of which are good."

Don't cut up your library with partitions unless you are sure they are absolutely necessary. Leave everything as open as possible. A light rail will keep intruders out of a private corner, and yet will not shut out light, or prevent circulation of air, or take away from the feeling of openness and breadth the library room ought to have.

For interior finish use few horizontal moldings; they make traps for dust. Use such shades at the windows as will permit adjustment for letting in light at top or bottom, or both. The less ornamentation in the furniture the better. A simple pine or white-wood table is more dignified and easier kept clean than a cheaply carved one of oak. But get solid, honestly-made, simple furniture of oak or similar wood, if funds permit. Arm-chairs are not often desirable. They take up much room, are heavy to move, and are not easy to get in and out of at a table. In many cases simple stools on a single iron standard, without a revolving top, fastened to the floor, are more desirable than chairs. The loafer doesn't like them; very few serious students object to them.

A stack room for small libraries is not advisable. Don't crowd your cases close together unless it is absolutely necessary.

An excellent form of wooden case is one seven feet high, with shelves three feet long and seven and a half inches wide, supported on iron pegs. The pegs fit into a series of holes bored one inch apart in the sides of the case, thus making the shelves adjustable. These pegs can be bought in the market in several shapes. The shelves have slots cut in the under side at the ends to hold the projecting ends of the pegs, thus giving no obstructions to the free movement of the books. With some forms of pegs the slots are not needed. The uprights are made of inch and a half stuff, or even inch and an eighth. The shelves are inch stuff, finished to seven-eighths of an inch. The backs are half inch stuff, tongued and grooved and put in horizontally. This case-unit (3' x 7' x 8") may be doubled or trebled, making cases six and nine feet long; or it may be made double-faced. If double-faced, and nine feet long, it will hold about a thousand books of ordinary size when full. It is often well to build several of your cases short and with a single front—wall cases—as they are when in this form more easily adjusted to the growing needs of the library.

A library can never do its best work until its management recognizes the duty and true economy of providing skilled assistants, comfortable quarters, and the best library equipment of fittings and supplies.

For cases, furniture, catalog cases, cards, trays, and labor-saving devices of all kinds, consult the catalog of the Library Bureau.

Very many libraries, even the smallest, find it advantageous to use for book cases what are known as "steel stacks." The demand for these cases has been so great from libraries, large and small, that shelving made from a combination of wood and steel has been very successfully adapted to this use, and at a price within the reach of all libraries. One of the principal advantages in buying such "steel stack" shelving, with parts all interchangeable, is that in the rearrangement of a room, or in moving into a new room or a new building, it can be utilized to advantage, whereas the common wooden book cases very generally cannot.

CHAPTER IX

Things needed in beginning work—Books, periodicals, and tools

The books and other things included in the following list—except those starred or excepted in a special note, the purchase of which can perhaps be deferred until the library contains a few thousand volumes—are essential to good work, and should be purchased, some of them as soon as a library is definitely decided upon, the others as soon as books are purchased and work is actually begun.

I. BOOKS

*American catalog of books in print from 1876-1896, 5v. with annual supplement. The Publishers' weekly, N. Y. Several of the volumes are out of print. All are expensive. They are not needed by the very small library. The recent years of the annual volumes are essential.

Card catalog rules; accessions-book rules; shelf-list rules; Library Bureau, 1899, $1.25. These are called the Library school rules.

Catalog of A. L. A. library; 5000v. for a popular library, selected by the American Library Association, and shown at the World's Columbian exhibition, Washington, 1893. Sent free from the United States Bureau of education.

*English catalog, 1835-1896, 5v., with annual supplement. The annual supplements for recent years are needed by the small library; the others are not.

Five thousand books, an easy guide to books in every department. Compiled for the Ladies' home journal, 1895. Curtis Publishing Company, Philadelphia, Pa. Paper, 10 cents. Out of print, but can probably be found second-hand.

Fletcher, W. I. Public Libraries in America, 1894. Roberts Bros., Boston, $1.

Library Bureau catalog, containing list of library tools, fittings, and appliances of all kinds, 1898. To be obtained of the Library Bureau, Chicago, 215 Madison St.; Boston, 530 Atlantic Ave.; New York, 250 Broadway; Philadelphia, 112 N. Broad St.; Washington, 1416 F St., N. W.

Plummer, M. W. Hints to small libraries, 1898. Truslove & Comba, N. Y., 50 cents.

Public library handbook, by the Public library, Denver, 1894. Carson, Harper Co., Denver, Col., $1.

Publishers' trade list annual, 1898, v. 26. Office of the Publishers' weekly, N. Y., $2. Catalogs of all important American publishers bound together in one volume.

Reference catalog of current literature, 1898. Catalogs of English publishers, bound in one volume and indexed. J. Whitaker & Sons, London, $5.

Rules for an author and title catalog, condensed. See Cutter, Rules for a dictionary catalog, 1891, p. 99-103. Sent from the United States Bureau of education, Washington, free. These are the rules adopted by the American Library Association.

*Sonnenschein, W. S. Best books, readers' guide, 1891. Sonnenschein, London, $8. Gives author, title, publisher and price of about 50,000 carefully selected and carefully classified books.

Sonnenschein, W. S. Reader's guide to contemporary literature (50,000v.), supplement to Best books, 1895. Sonnenschein, London, $6.50.

*Subject headings for use in dictionary catalogs, Library Bureau, 1898, $2. In a small library this is not needed, but it will save trouble to get it.

Lawrence, I. Classified reading. A list with publishers and prices of books for the school, the library, and the home, 1898. Normal school, St Cloud, Minn., $1.25.

Iles, George. List of books for girls and women and their clubs, 1895. Library Bureau, $1.

World's library congress, papers prepared for, held at World's Columbian exposition, Chicago, 1893. United States Bureau of education, Washington, D. C., free. Covers very fully the entire field of library economy.

II. PERIODICALS

Book news, monthly. Wanamaker, Philadelphia, 50 cents. (Book reviews.)

Dial, semi-monthly, 24 Adams St., Chicago, $2. (Book reviews, notes and essays.)

Literature, weekly. Harper & Bros., N. Y., $4. (Current English and American literature.)

Nation, weekly. New York, $3. (Book reviews, art, politics.)

Publishers' weekly, the American book trade journal, 59 Duane St., N. Y., $5. (Lists nearly all American and best English books as published.)

Library journal, monthly, $5 a year, 58 Duane St., New York. This is the official organ of the American Library Association.

Public libraries, monthly, $1 a year, 215 Madison

St., Chicago. Presents library methods in a manner especially helpful to small libraries.

New York Times Saturday review of books and art. The Times, N. Y., $1.

Monthly cumulative book index. An author, title, and subject index to the books published during the current year, brought up to date in one alphabet each month. Morris & Wilson, Minneapolis, Minn., $1.50.

III. OTHER THINGS

Accession book. See catalog of the Library Bureau. For a very small library a common blank-book will do.

Agreement blanks, which the borrower signs before getting his borrower's card giving him the right to use the library. See chapter on charging systems.

Book cards. See chapter on charging systems, and Library Bureau catalog.

Book pockets. See Library Bureau catalog, and also chapter on charging systems.

Borrowers' cards. Given to borrowers as evidence of their right to draw books. See chapter on charging systems.

Borrowers' register, best kept on cards. See chapter on charging systems.

Catalog cards. These are of two sizes and many thicknesses. Select what suits you. See Library Bureau catalog.

Catalog case. See Library Bureau catalog. For a very small library a few japanned tin trays will serve. But your catalog will grow faster than you suppose.

Cole size card; a sheet marked in such a way as to give one at a glance the proper letter to use in indicating the size of any book placed on it. See Library

Bureau catalog. In a very small library not needed.

Classification scheme. See chapters on classification.

Cutter author table for book numbers. See chapter on book numbers. For a very small library one can use numbers only.

Daters and ink pads for dating borrowers' cards, etc. The pencil daters are best. See chapter on charging systems.

Ink. For all outside labels use Higgins' American drawing ink, waterproof. For book cards, borrowers' cards, etc., use any good black, non-copying ink. Carter's fluid is very good.

Labels. Round ones are best and those ready gummed do well if carefully put on. Dennison's "88A" are good.

Paste. Binder's paste is good; for library use it needs thinning. Higgins' photo mounter and other like bottled pastes are better.

Rubber stamps and ink pad for marking books with name of library. See chapter on preparing books for the shelves.

Shelf list cards. See Library Bureau catalog.

Shelf list sheets (or cards). See Library Bureau catalog. In a very small library sheets of ordinary ruled writing paper will serve. It is better, however, to get the right thing at the start.

CHAPTER X

The relation of the Library Bureau to libraries

Geo. B. Meleney, Ch. Mgr., in Public Libraries, May, 1896

The consideration of the relations of the Library Bureau to libraries brings us back to the organization of the American Library Association in 1876. At this gathering of the prominent librarians of the country, the discussion of methods brought out the lack of unanimity in, and the need of coöperation for, a uniform system in the various branches of library work. To carry out uniform methods requires uniform material, and this was hard to obtain. The American Library Association as such, of course, could not take up a business venture of this kind, but it was decided to advise an organization for keeping on sale such supplies and library aids as the association might decide were needed.

The Library Bureau was then organized for this purpose, and has continued to keep the same relation toward the library association as was originally intended. Referring to the numbers of the Library Bureau catalogs, one may trace the history of the development not only of the appliances furnished by the Library Bureau, but also of ideas of library economy as they are gathered there from every source. It confined its attention at first to libraries only, the business being divided into four departments: employment, to bring together libraries and librarians; consultation, to give expert advice on any phase of any library question;

publication, to publish the various needed helps (from point of usefulness to libraries rather than profit to publishers); supply, to furnish at lower prices all articles recommended by the A. L. A., and to equip any library with best known devices in everything needful. Among the things noticed in these departments are catalog cards, cases, trays, and outfits, book supports, blanks, book pockets, boxes, desks, inks, etc. Some specialties are noted in library devices, and helpful advice as to their economical use is given. The successive catalogs follow the same line, attention being directed toward all improvements in old material, and to all advanced work in library administration wherever found. Not all the material recommended was manufactured by the Library Bureau, but a generous spirit is shown in recommending any device, plan, or publication known to be helpful to the library profession. It has brought to notice many notable contributions to library literature, such as the Author table, by C. A. Cutter, of the Boston athenæum; Decimal classification and relative index and Library notes, by Melvil Dewey; *Library journal;* Library school rules; Perkins' manual; Linderfelt's rules; Sargent's Reading for the young; Lists of books for different clubs; Subject headings of A. L. A., etc. The Library Bureau catalog itself is one of the best library aids ever published. These catalogs have always been sent free to library workers.

Libraries grew in numbers and size largely because of the enthusiasm of earnest workers, but very frequently with hardly enough financial assistance to warrant more than the purchase of a few books, and frequently with limited knowledge of how to make the small store of use to the waiting public. The management of the Library Bureau at this time was certainly doing a missionary work; but its chief problem was the financial one, or how to make both ends meet, and it was not until library methods were introduced into business houses that this question was solved. The constant and untiring efforts of the management of the Library Bureau toward the assistance and upbuilding of the smaller and younger libraries have had much to do with the growth of library sentiment, which is now so apparent on every hand, and indirectly this knowledge of library work and library methods has done much to enlarge the facilities of the Library Bureau.

From a very unpretentious concern, publishing a few library aids, manufacturing such library devices as could not be obtained elsewhere, and keeping for sale a few articles of library furnishing, the Library Bureau has grown to be a corporation of no small proportions, having numerous branches both in this country and Europe, maintaining a card factory, cabinet works in Boston and Chicago, and facilities for the manufacture of steel stacks unexcelled in this country.

The Library Bureau, however, has never forgotten the cause of its birth or the teachings of its youth, as is clearly evidenced from year to year by the various undertakings and publications which a careful observer can clearly see are not put forward with any presage of success when viewed entirely from a business standpoint. This lesson is constantly taught to the employés of the Library Bureau, and they are positively instructed that, regardless of the promise of success in other directions, the attention to library requirements is the first demand.

The Library Bureau maintains at its various offices persons thoroughly versed in library economy, for the express purpose of furnishing detailed information and aid to those younger members of the profession whom they have the pleasure and opportunity of assisting over the stumbling-blocks in their daily work. With this same idea in view it publishes from the Chicago office a monthly magazine called PUBLIC LIBRARIES, of an elementary character, which is entertaining, instructive, and inspiring, and helps to encourage a sentiment favorable to public libraries and to make librarianship a profession of high standing.

CHAPTER XI

Selecting books—Fitting the library to its owners

The selection of books should be left to the librarian, under the general direction of trustees or book committee.

There should be made at the start a collection of encyclopedias, dictionaries, gazetteers, and scientific compendiums, which should not be lent. The extent of this collection will depend on the scope and purposes of the library. No library, however small, can dispense with some books of reference. But for a small library don't buy expensive works. The Encyclopædia Britannica is an example of what not to get.

There must be taken into consideration, in determining the character of the books to be purchased, these factors among others:

a) Presence or absence of other libraries in the vicinity, and their character, if present.

b) The avowed purposes of the free, tax-supported public library, to-wit: 1) To help people to be happy; 2) to help them to become wise; 3) to encourage them to be good.

c) The amount of money to be expended and the sum that will probably be available for each succeeding year.

d) The manner in which the books are to be used; whether they are to be lent, or are to be used only for reference, or are to form both a reference and a lending library.

e) The class of people by whom they are to be used, and if children, whether for school work only, or for general reading, or for both.

f) The occupations and leading local interests of the community.

g) The character and average degree of intelligence of the community.

h) The habits, as to reading and study, of those who will use the library.

The village library, in its early days, can well afford to begin at the level of the community's average reading. At the same time it must always try to go a little ahead of the demands of the people, and develop a taste and desire for the very best books it can get. The masses of the people have very little of literary culture. It is the purpose of the public library to develop this by creating in them the habit of reading. As a rule people read books which are above their own intellectual and moral standard, and hence are benefited by reading. The reading of books generally leads to the reading of better books.

Then do not aim too high. Avoid trash, but do not buy literature which will not be read simply because it is standard or classic. Remember that the public library is a popular institution in every sense of the word; that it has become possible only by the approval of the majority of the population, and that the majority of the population is confined in its turn to a majority of people of the most commonplace kind.

Do not pander to any sect, creed, or partisan taste. Buy largely books costing from 50 cents to $2, found in so many of the series now published. These are fresh, up-to-date, written for the most part by competent men, and are reliable. They are not dull, because no one can afford to be dull in a 12mo volume. As a general thing they are well made, supplied with maps and illustrations when needed, and have indexes. Put much of your money into the history, travel, and literature of your own country first, and then see what you have left for Greece and Rome. The common people nowadays should be encouraged in their interest in their own country, its description, history, politics, biography, mineral resources, literature. The people will inquire for these books, and they should be provided for them. Wait until the library is larger before investing much money in the history of worn out empires, simply because such and such a person wants them, or because some library anywhere from two to twenty times as large has them. Use common sense and much of it.

Put into the people's hands books worthy of their respect, then insist that they be handled carefully and treated always with consideration. Expensive books; that is, books which are first-class in paper, ink, and binding, are generally better worth their cost than cheap ones.

In the first purchases buy largely for children. They are the library's best pupils. They are more easily trained to enjoy good books than their elders. Through them the homes are best reached. They will, by their free use of the library, and by their approval of it, do much to add to its popularity. The best books for children will be enjoyed by all.

In selecting fiction, get from the older librarians a statement of what are the most popular of the wholesome novels found on their shelves. A better guide than this it will be difficult to find. Fiction is of the greatest value in developing a taste for reading. Everyone should be familiar with the great works of imagination. Nearly all the greatest literature of the world is fiction. The educational value of the novel is not often questioned.

But don't buy a novel simply because it is popular. If you follow that line you will end with the cheapest kind of stuff. Some librarians pretend that they must buy to please the public taste; that they can't use their own judgment in selecting books for a library which the public purse supports. Why these librarians don't supply the Police gazette it is difficult to understand. "The public" would like it—some of them. We select school committees and superintendents and teachers to run our schools. We ask them to inform themselves on the subject and give us the best education they can. They don't try to suit everybody. They try to furnish the best. Library trustees and librarian are in a like case. The silly, the weak, the sloppy, the wishy-washy novel, the sickly love story, the belated tract, the crude hodge-podge of stilted conversation, impossible incident, and moral platitude or moral bosh for children—these are not needed. It is as bad to buy them and circulate them, knowingly, as it would be for our school authorities to install in our schoolrooms as teachers romantic, giggling girls and smarty boys. Buy good novels, those the wise approve of, in good type, paper, and binding; keep plenty of copies of each on hand; put them where your readers can handle them; add a few each year of the best only of the latest novels, and those chiefly on trial (not to be bought again if found not to have real merit) and your public will be satisfied, and your library will be all the time raising the taste of the community.

Some books should not be put, at least not without comment, into the hands of young people. Other books, some people think, should not be read by young people. Other books, some people think, should not be in a public library at all. A good course to follow in regard to such books is to consider the temper of your community and put into the library as many of them as are noteworthy in a literary way as your public will permit and your resources permit.

In other departments follow at first the guidance of some one of the good book lists now available.

Books on zoölogy, geology, and botany should be by American in preference to foreign authors. In all departments select the latest editions, and, at first, the recent book rather than the older book.

The proportion of books in the different departments of knowledge must vary greatly in different libraries. The following is a good general guide:

	Per cent.
General works	.04
Philosophy	.01
Religion	.02
Sociology	.09
Philology	.01
Science	.08
Useful arts	.06
Fine arts	.04
Literature	.12
Biography	.10
History	.13
Travels	.10
Fiction	.20
Total	100

Local interest should be fostered by buying freely books on local history and science and books by local authors.

The librarian should keep informed of coming events, and see that the library is provided with the books for which there is sure to be a future demand. He should avoid personal hobbies and be impartial on all controversial questions. He should not be over-confident in his knowledge of what will elevate and refine the community.

It is better to buy 10 extra copies of a wholesome book wanted by the public than one copy each of 10 other books which will not be read.

Do not waste time, energy, and money—certainly not in the early days of the library—in securing or arranging public documents, save a few of purely local value. Take them if offered and store them.

Do not be too much impressed by the local history plea, and spend precious money on rare volumes or old journals in this line.

Certain work can judiciously be done toward collecting and preserving materials for local history that will involve neither expense nor much labor, and this the librarian should do. Do not turn the public library, which is chiefly to be considered as a branch of a live, everyday system of popular education, into a local antiquarian society; but simply let it serve incidentally as a picker-up of unconsidered trifles. A wide-awake, scholarly librarian will like his town, and delight in at least some study of its antecedents. And such a librarian need not be a crank, but must needs be an enterprising, wide-awake, appreciative student, who can scent the tastes and needs of posterity.

Put no money into rare books. A book which was out of print 10 years or 200 years ago, and has not insisted upon republication since, has, ordinarily, no place in the active, free public library. If you get it, sell it and buy a live book.

The free public library should encourage its readers to suggest books not in the library, by providing blanks for that purpose, and paying courteous attention to all requests.

Ask by letter, by circulars, and by notes in the local papers, for gifts of books, money, and periodicals. Acknowledge every gift. Remember that one who has helped the library, be it ever so little, has thereby become interested in it, and is its friend.

CHAPTER XII

Reference books for a small library, compiled by C. A. Baker, of the Public library, Denver

This list includes about 75 books, costing about $550. It is arranged alphabetically. It is subdivided into four lists, arranged according to relative importance. This subdivision is shown by the numbers prefixed to each entry.

2. Adams, C. K. Manual of historical literature. 1889. O. Harper, cl. $2.50.

1. Adams, O. F. Dictionary of American authors. 1897. O. Houghton, Mifflin, cl. $3.

1. Adler, G. J. Dictionary of the German and English languages. 1893. Q. Appleton, mor. $5.

4. Allibone, S. A. Critical dictionary of English literature. 1891, 3v. Q. Lippincott, sh. $22.50.

4. Allibone, S. A. Supplement to the critical dictionary of English literature, by J. F. Kirk. 1892, 2v. Q. Lippincott, sh. $15.

1. Appleton's annual cyclopædia and register of important events. Q. Appleton, cl. $5.

3. Appleton's cyclopædia of American biography. 1888–92, 6v. Q. Appleton, cl. $30, half mor. $42.

1. Appleton's cyclopædia of applied mechanics, ed. by P. Benjamin. 1893, 2v. Q. Appleton, sh. $15, half mor. $17.

2. Appleton's modern mechanism, supplement to Cyclopædia of applied mechanics. 1892, 1v. Q. Appleton, sh. $7.50, half mor. $8.50.

2. Bartlett, J., ed. Familiar quotations. 1892. O. Little, cl. $3.

3. Bliss, E. M., ed. Cyclopædia of missions, 2v. 1891. Q. Funk & Wagnalls, cl. $12.

1. Bliss, W. D. P. Cyclopædia of social reform, including political economy, science, sociology, statistics, anarchism, charities, civil service, currency, land, etc. 1897. Q. Funk & Wagnalls, cl. $7.50, sh. $9.50.

3. Brannt, W. T. and Wahl, W. H. Technico-chemical receipt book. 1895. D. Baird, cl. $2.

1. Brewer, E. C. Reference library, 1885-98. 4v. O. Lippincott. $13. Dictionary of miracles, Historic notebook, Dictionary of phrase and fable, Reader's handbook.

2. Brown, E. and Strauss, A. Dictionary of American politics. 1895. D. Burt, cl., $1.

1. Bryant, W. C., ed. Library of poetry and song. 1876. Q. Fords, Howard, cl., $5.

3. Century dictionary and cyclopædia. (Century dictionary and the Century cyclopædia of names combined with the atlas of the world.) 10v. Prices from $60 to $150. Often can be picked up second-hand.

1. Century atlas of the world. 1897. F. Century Co., cl. $12.50, half mor. $15.

1. Century cyclopædia of names, n. d. F. Century Co., cl. $10.50, buf. $12.50.

(Note.—The two last are included in the Century dictionary and cyclopædia, but can be bought separately.)

2. Chambers, R., ed. Book of days, 2v. O. Lippincott. 1893. $7.

2. Champlin, J. D. jr. Young folks' cyclopædia of common things. 1893. O. Holt, cl. $2.50.

2. Champlin, J. D. jr. Young folks' cyclopædia of persons and places. 1892. O. Holt, cl. $2.50.

2. Champlin, J. D. jr. and Bostwick, A. E. Young folks' cyclopædia of games and sports. 1890. O. Holt, cl. $2.50.

2. Channing, E. and Hart, A. B. Guide to the study of American history. O. Ginn. 1896. $2.

1. Clement, C. E. Painters, architects, engravers, and their work. 1881. D. Houghton, Mifflin, cl. $3. (Artists not living.)

1. Clement, C. E. and Hutton, L. Artists of the 19th century and their work. 1885 D. Houghton & Mifflin, cl. $3.

4. Cram's Bankers and brokers' railroad atlas; complete alphabetical index. 1898. F. Cram. $17.50.

1. Cumulative index of periodicals, monthly and annual. 1898. Helman-Taylor Co., Cleveland, pa. $5.

4. Cyclopædia of American biographies. J. H. Brown, ed. 1897. v. 1, A-C. Q. Cyclo. Pub. Co., Boston, half mor. $7.

2. Fields, J. T. and Whipple, E. P., ed. Family library of British poetry. 1882. Q. Houghton, cl. $5, mor. $10.

3. Fletcher, W. I., ed. A. L. A. index to general literature. 1893. Q. Houghton, cl. $5.

1. Fletcher, W. I., ed., and Bowker, R. R. Annual literary index, including periodicals and essays. 1899. O. Publishers' weekly, cl. $3.50.

3. Frey, A. R. Sobriquets and nicknames. 1888. O. Houghton, cl. $2.

1. Goodholme, T. S. Domestic encyclopædia of practical information. 1889. O. Scribners, cl. $5.

1. Harper's book of facts. C. T. Lewis, ed. 1895. Q. Harper. Sub. only, $8.

3. Harper's cyclopædia of British and American

poetry. E. Sargent, ed. 1881. Q. Harper, hf. leather, $5.

2. Harper's dictionary of classical literature and antiquities. H. T. Peck, ed. 1897. Q. Harper, cl. $6.

4. Hastings, J. Dictionary of the Bible, 4v. O. 1898. Clark, cl. 28s per vol., half mor. 34s. per vol.

3. Haydn's dictionary of dates. B. Vincent, ed. 1895. O. Putnam, cl. $6, half mor. $9.

2. Hazell's annual; record of men and topics of the day. 1899. D. Hazell, 3s. 6d.

2. Hopkins, A. A. Scientific American cyclopædia of receipts, notes, and queries. 1892. O. cl. $5, sh. $6.

1. Hoyt, J. K. Cyclopædia of practical quotations, English, Latin, and modern foreign. 1896. Q. Funk & Wagnalls, cl. $5, sh. $8.

1. Jameson, J. F. Dictionary of United States history, 1492-1894. 1894. Q. Puritan Pub., cl. $2.75, half mor. $3.50.

1. Johnson's universal cyclopædia. 1893, 8v. Q. Johnson, half mor. $56, cl. $48.

2. King, M., ed. Handbook of the United States. 1891. O. King (Matthews, Northrop Co.), cl. $2.50.

3. Larned, J. N., ed. History for ready reference, from the best historians, biographers, and specialists. 1894. 5v. Maps. Nichols Co., Springfield, Mass. cl. $5 each, half mor. $6 each.

2. Lalor, J. J., ed. Cyclopædia of political science, political economy, and political history of the United States. 1890-93. 3v. Q. C. E. Merrill, $15.

1. Leypoldt, A. H. and Iles, G. List of books for girls and women. Dewey classification numbers with each entry. 1895. Library Bureau, cl. $1.

1. Lippincott's gazetteer of the world. 1896. Q. Lippincott, sh. $8.

4. Lippincott's universal pronouncing dictionary of biography and mythology, by J. Thomas. 1892. Q. Lippincott, in IV., sh. $8, half turkey $11; in 2v., sh. $10.

2. Lossing, B. J. Popular cyclopædia of United States history. 1893. 2v. Q. Harper, mor. $15.

3. Lübke, W. Outlines of the history of art. 1891. 2v. O. Dodd, Mead, half roan, $7.50.

1. Matson, H. References for literary workers. 1893. O. McClurg, $2.50.

1. Men and women of the time. 14th ed. 1895. O. Routledge. $5.

3. Mineral industry, its statistics, technology, and trade, ed. by R. R. Rothwell, annual. O. Scientific Pub. Co., cl. $5.

2. Mulhall, M. G. Dictionary of statistics. 1898. Ed. 4. Q. Routledge, cl. $8.

3. Mulhall, M. G. Industries and wealth of nations. 1896. O. Longman, cl. $3.

1. Patrick, D. and Gromme, F. H., eds. Chambers biographical dictionary. 1898. O. Lippincott, half mor. $3.50.

4. Poole, W. F. and Fletcher, W. Poole's index to periodical literature. O. Houghton, Mifflin.

 V. 1. in two parts, cl. $16, sh. $24.
 V. 2. Jan. 1882– Jan. 1887. cl. $8, sh. $10.
 V. 3. Jan. 1887– Jan. 1892. cl. $8, sh. $12.
 V. 4. Jan. 1892– Jan. 1897. cl. $10, sh. $12.

In a small library having bound periodicals of recent date only, volume 4 alone is sufficient.

1. Rand-McNally indexed atlas of the world. 1897. 2v. 58x41 cm. Rand-McNally. cl. $18.50, half leather, $23.50.

3. Riemann, H. Dictionary of music. O. Augenev, $3.75.

2. Smith, H. P. and Johnson, H. K. Dictionary of terms, phrases, and quotations. 1895. O. Appleton, half leather, $3.

3. Smith, W. Classical dictionary. New edition by Marindin. 1894. O. Appleton, $6.

1. Smith, W. Dictionary of the Bible. 1884. O. Coates, cl. $2, half mor. $3.

3. Smith, W. and Cheetham, S. Dictionary of Christian antiquities. 1891. 2v. O. Burr, Hartford, Conn., cl. $7, leather $8.

1. Soule, R. Dictionary of English synonyms. 1895. O. Lippincott, cl. $2.25, mor. $2.75.

1. Spiers, A. and Surenne, O. French and English pronouncing dictionary. 1891. Q. Appleton, half mor. $5.

1. Standard dictionary of the English language, 2v. Q. 1895. Funk & Wagnalls, half rus. $15; with Denison's reference index, $17.

3. Statesmen's year book, 1899, v. 36. D. Macmillan, $3.

2. Walsh, W. S. Handy book of literary curiosities. 1893. O. Lippincott, half leather, $3.50.

2. Walsh, W. S. Curiosities of popular customs, and of rites, ceremonies, observances and miscellaneous antiquities. 1898. O. Lippincott, half leather, $3.50.

1. Webster, N. International dictionary. Springfield, Mass. Merriam. 1891. $10.

2. Wheeler, W. A. Familiar allusions. 1891. D. Houghton, cl. $2.

2. Wheeler, W. A. Explanatory and pronouncing

dictionary of noted names of fiction. 1892. D. Houghton, cl. $2.

3. Wheeler, W. A. and C. G. Who wrote it? D. Lee & Shepard, cl. $2.

2. Whitaker's almanac. 1899. D. Whitaker, paper, 2s. 6d.

Whitaker's directory of titled persons for the year 1898; a companion to his Almanac. D. Whitaker, paper, 2s. 6d.

3. Who's who? annual; autobiographies of the leading men and women of the day; complete peerage, etc. 1899. D. Black, cl. 3s. 6d.

1. World almanac and encyclopædia. 1898. D. New York World, pa. 25 cents.

2. Young, R. Analytical concordance to the Bible, n. d. Ed. 6. Q. Religious tract society, cl. 24s., mor. 30s.

CHAPTER XIII

Reference work—Helping the inexperienced inquirer—Periodicals

Reference work in libraries large and small has for its first rule: Meet the inquirer more than half way. To the stranger a library is often an oppressive place, an awesome place—in his imagination. He comes in shyly; everyone appears busy, his question suddenly seems to him trivial; he won't trouble these wise and busy people with it—and goes out.

A good second rule is: Learn at once just exactly what the inquirer wishes to know. This is not always easy. Tact and a little patience will generally effect it.

A good third rule is: Whenever possible show the inquirer how the answer is found, so that he may next time in some measure help himself. It is surprising how many, especially of the younger people in a community, can be taught within one year, on their occasional visits, to make the proper use of at least a few reference books.

Another rule of very general application is: Go first to a dictionary. In many cases a question answers itself, or betrays where its answer may best be found, if it is once plainly stated. And nothing is better than reference to a few words in a dictionary for the clear statement of a question. The larger dictionaries, moreover, and notably the Century, will answer many more inquiries than even great readers often suppose.

Many questions come up again and again. Of

these, and of the references which answered them, notes should be kept on cards for future use. In fact it is well to keep an index in this way of the references looked up for all the more important inquiries.

The following excellent advice is from an article on The use of periodicals in reference work, by Frederick Winthrop Faxon, in Public Libraries for June, 1898:

"In all reference work periodicals play a large part. They may be roughly divided into two great classes, the technical and the popular. The former are indispensable to the scholar, or the expert, and in the rapid advancement of science are the only real sources of information. Text-books or treatises are out of date before published; therefore for a correct present view, or a complete history of the development of any science, the technical reviews and society transactions must be consulted. These will be the principal part of a scientific library, and should be in the large public and college libraries in order to cover advanced study. They have, on the other hand, little place in small libraries—they would seldom be of use, and are very expensive.

"But the popular periodicals every library needs. In the better class of these reviews it is possible, if we know where to look, to find several articles on both sides of almost any subject. Furthermore, these are often written by the foremost authors or scientists, and are in a language intelligible to all. The amateur cannot give the time or patience to wade two-volume deep in the subject his club wishes him to treat in half an hour's speech. The magazine gives just what he wants in several pages. There are periodicals exclusively devoted to every branch of every science, and magazines which, in their files, include articles on all subjects. This mine of information has been opened up by Poole's index. Since 1881, when the third and enlarged edition of Poole's index was published, all this is common property for the asking. Grouped around Poole and keeping pace with the times are the Poole supplements, which ought, perhaps, to be named the Fletchers, covering the five-year periods since 1881, ending respectively 1886, 1891, 1896. Then the Annual literary index gives a yearly index of subjects and authors, and serves as a supplement to the Poole supplement. For such as cannot be even a year without a periodical index we now have the admirable Cumulative index, bi-monthly, edited by the Cleveland public library. Thus all the principal periodicals since the beginning of the century may be consulted by reference to one or more of five single books or alphabets.

"The Review of reviews must be mentioned as a useful monthly index to current periodical literature, but of little value for study reference as compared with the indexes just mentioned. An annual index issued by the Review of reviews, since 1890, is good in its way, though rather superficial. Sargent's Reading for the young, and its supplement, index the juvenile sets of St Nicholas, Harper's young people, and Wide Awake. Poole and the Cumulative are of little use without a fair assortment of the sets therein indexed.

"Thus far 442 titles (practically all of them serials published since 1800) have been indexed. It is a mistake, however, to suppose that most of these are necessary in a small library before Poole's index should be purchased or can be of use. Given Poole and a complete set of Littell's living age, and Harper's monthly, more reference work can be done than with twice the number of reference books not periodicals. A small collection of sets has enabled more than one struggling library to hold its own with the students and club members, and to accomplish work which could not have been done as well with many works of reference, the purchase of which would have exhausted the whole book fund."

CHAPTER XIV

Reading room—Periodicals

A free reading room is generally opened in connection with the library, and often proves its most attractive feature. It should be comfortably furnished and scrupulously clean. As the room is for the use of all clean and orderly people, quiet should be maintained to give all a chance to read and study without interruption. There should be no signs commanding things, and the fewest possible—and they unobtrusive—requesting things. Signs giving information helpful to readers are always permissible; but see that they harmonize with the furnishings of the room and are clean. Gray, or some modest tint, is preferable to white cardboard for all signs. The general atmosphere of the place should be such as one would wish to have in his own home—orderly, inviting, cheerful.

The village library ought to preserve for reference a file of local papers; and it seems proper for it to provide for public use a few dailies or weeklies from the nearest cities. Further than this in this direction it would not seem expedient to go, because better work can be done, with the money newspapers would cost, in other directions. In fact, where the room is limited, as well as funds, it will often be better to provide no newspapers at all. Few are unable to get papers to read elsewhere. The library can well devote itself to the encouraging the reading of other things. Most people read the newspapers enough, library or no library.

Many, save for the library, would not read the standard American and English periodicals.

The young people are the library's most hopeful material. To them the librarian hopes to give, through books and journals, an added pleasure; and in them he hopes to awaken a taste for reading something—in time something good. To attract the children it will be wise to have on file a few juvenile journals and picture papers and illustrated magazines. As to the standard and popular monthlies and quarterlies there seems to be no question; they should be taken freely. The

Magazine binder. (Reduced; various sizes.)

magazines furnish us with the best fiction, the best poetry, the best essays, the best discussions of all subjects, old and new, and the latest science. It is a question if many a village library would not do more, vastly more, to stimulate the mental life of its community, and to broaden its views and sympathies, and to encourage study, if it diverted a far larger part of its income than it now does from inferior books, and especially inferior novels, to weekly journals and popular and standard magazines. It is not yet fully impressed upon us that the thing the community needs is not a "library"—it may have a street lined with "libraries" and still dwell in the outer darkness—but contact with the printed page. Get this contact first, then, by means of attractive rooms, and clean, wholesome, interesting periodicals and books, and let the well rounded students' collection of books come on as it will.

From 5 to 20 per cent can very often be saved on the cost of periodicals by ordering them through a reliable subscription agency.

The custom is extending of taking extra numbers of the popular magazines and lending them as if they were books, though generally for a shorter period and without the privilege of renewal. When this is done, put each magazine in a binder made for the purpose, and marked with the library's name, to keep it clean and smooth, and to identify it as library property. Similar binders are often put on the magazines which are placed in the reading rooms. (See Library Bureau catalog.)

Complete volumes of the magazines are in great demand with the borrowing public. The magazine indexes now available will make useful to the student the smallest library's supply of periodical literature.

In small reading rooms the periodicals that are supplied should be placed on tables where readers can consult them without application to the attendants. Files and racks for newspapers, special devices for holding illustrated journals, and other things of like nature, are to be found in great variety.

Post up in the reading room a list of the periodicals regularly received; also a list of those in the bound files.

A careful record should be kept of each magazine ordered, of the date when ordered, the date when the subscription begins and expires, the price paid, the agency from which it is ordered, and the date of that agency's receipted bill. If the list of journals taken is small this record can be kept very conveniently in a blank book. If it is large and constantly growing or changing, it is best kept on cards, a card to each journal, and all alphabetically arranged. It saves much trouble when dealing with an agency to have subscriptions coincide with the calendar year, disregarding the volume arrangements of the publishers.

CHAPTER XV

List of periodicals for a small library

[See also chapter List of things needed in beginning work.]

Century magazine (monthly), illus. N. Y. Century Co. Ed. by R. W. Gilder, $4.
Harper's new monthly magazine, illus. N. Y. Harper. Ed. by H. M. Alden, $4.
Harper's round table (monthly), illus. N. Y. Harper, $1.
St Nicholas (monthly), illus. N. Y. Century Co. Ed. by Mary Mapes Dodge, $3.
Forum (monthly), N. Y. Forum Co., $3.
Harper's weekly, illus. N. Y. Harper, $4.
Youth's companion (weekly). Boston. Perry Mason Co., $1.75.
McClure's magazine (monthly), illus. N. Y. Doubleday & McClure, $1.
Ladies' home journal (monthly), illus. Phila. Curtis Pub. Co., $1.
Independent (weekly). N. Y. $2.
Outlook (weekly), illus. N. Y. $3.
Engineering magazine (monthly). N. Y. $3.
Life (weekly), illus. N. Y. $5.
Nineteenth century (monthly). N. Y. Leonard Scott Co., $4.50.
Review of reviews (monthly), illus. N. Y. Ed. by Albert Shaw, $2.50.
Contemporary review (monthly). N. Y. Leonard Scott Co., $4.50.

Critic (monthly), illus. N. Y. Critic Co., $2.
Nation (weekly). N. Y. Evening Post Co., $3.
Educational review (monthly), N. Y. Holt, $3.
Kindergarten magazine (monthly), illus. Chicago Kindergarten Literature Co., $2.
Appleton's popular science monthly, illus. N. Y. Appleton, $5.
Scientific American (weekly), illus. N. Y. Munn, $3. With supplement, $7.
Scientific American supplement (weekly), illus. N. Y. Munn, $5.
Art amateur (monthly), illus. N. Y. Montague Marks, $4.
Outing (monthly), illus. N. Y. Outing Co., $3.

CHAPTER XVI

Buying books

A good book for a library, speaking of the book as to its wearing qualities and as to the comfort of its users, is printed on paper which is thin and pliable, but tough and opaque. Its type is not necessarily large, but is clear-cut and uniform, and set forth with ink that is black, not muddy. It is well bound, the book opening easily at any point. The threads in the back are strong and generously put in. The strings or tapes onto which it is sewn are stout, and are laced into the inside edges of the covers, or are strong enough to admit of a secure fastening with paste and paper. In ordering books of which several editions are on the market, specify the edition you wish. When you have found a good edition of a popular author like Scott or Dickens, make a note of it on the shelf-list.

In giving your orders, always try your local dealer first. If he cannot give you good terms, or, as is very likely to be the case, has not the information or the facilities which enable him to serve you well, submit a copy of the list to several large book dealers, choosing those nearest your town, and ask for their discounts. It is economical, generally, to purchase all your books through one dealer, thus saving letter writing, misunderstandings, freight, express, and general discomfort.

Keep a record of all books ordered. The best form of record is on slips, using a separate slip for each book. These order slips should have on them the author's surname, brief title, number of volumes, abbreviated note of place, publisher, year, publisher's price if known, name of dealer of whom ordered, date when ordered, and if its purchase has been requested by anyone that person's name and address.

For transmitting the order to the book dealer, a list on sheets should be made from the order slips, arranged either by publishers or alphabetically by authors. This list may be written on one side of the paper only, with copying ink, and a letter-press copy

Simple form of order slip on plain paper. (Reduced; actual size, 7½ x 12½ cm.)

taken; or, make a carbon copy of the sheet sent to the dealer. The carbon copy has the advantage of being easier to handle and better to write on. The books as received should be checked by this copy, or by the order cards. The cards for books received should be put by themselves, alphabetically, and kept until the books they represent have been cataloged and the cards for them have been properly entered in the card catalog. You thus will have lists 1) of books ordered and not received; 2) of books received and not cataloged; 3) of books cataloged. If few books are bought this work is unnecessary.

Books will often be ordered at the request of interested persons. In such cases the name and address of the person asking for the book should be entered on the bottom of the order slip for that book. When the book comes, and has been made ready for use, send a note to this person, notifying him of the fact of its arrival.

Do not be tempted by a large discount to give orders to irresponsible persons. A library should secure from 25 to 35 per cent discount. Do not buy ordinary subscription books or books on the installment plan. Do not anticipate revenues, and do not spend all your

Order slip. (Reduced; actual size, 7½ x 12½ cm.)

money at once; if you do you will miss many a bargain, and have to go without books that are needed more than those you have bought. Buy good but not expensive editions. Do not spend on a single costly work, of interest to few and seldom used by that few, a sum that would buy 20 or perhaps 100 volumes that would be in constant and profitable use by many. Buy no book unless by personal acquaintance, or upon competent and trustworthy testimony, it is worth adding to your library. Do not feel that you must buy complete sets of an author, or all of any "series"; all the works of very few authors are worth having. Do not buy cheap editions of fiction; the paper, presswork, and binding is poor, and is simply a waste of money. The best is none too good in buying fiction, for it wears out fast, and has to be rebound, and then replaced. Do not buy a lot of second-hand fiction to put into the hands of the people. You cannot expect them to keep their books clean if you start them out with dirty pages, soiled plates, and a general hand-me-down air.

Books for young people must be interesting. No amount of excellence in other directions will compensate for dull books.

Do not trust too much to the second-hand dealer; his wares are often defective. Do not buy of a book peddler; in nine cases out of ten you can find better and cheaper books at the stores. A well selected and judiciously purchased library, with such works of reference as are needed, will cost, on an average, $1.25 a volume.

The following notes were prepared by a bookseller of experience, and should be carefully considered before beginning to buy books:

Any bookseller worthy your patronage will be able to assist you by pointing out the most desirable edition for general library use.

There is every reason for placing your orders with your local dealer so long as he can care for them intelligently. A large discount should not be the sole factor in deciding where to buy, but keep in mind this, a conscientious bookseller can save you money by carefully watching your interests in the very many details that pertain to bookbuying. Having decided on your bookseller agent, place all your orders with him. It will save you time, which is equivalent to money. Keep an exact duplicate copy of every order you place, and for this purpose a manifold book is preferable. In writing your orders never write on both sides of a sheet; arrange your items alphabetically by author, and make all your entries as complete and full as possible. This is particularly important in the case of books in the field of science, history, and biography. The more clear and definite your orders are made out, the more promptly and completely can your bookseller supply them.

An ideal bookseller, qualified to act as your agent, is one who has familiarized himself with the various editions of books, and will always make selections with greater stress on quality than quantity; who will not send you the second edition of a scientific work when a third is out; who will avoid sending you expensive publications (even though you may have ordered them) until he is satisfied that you want them; who will exert himself to get desirable books that may be out of print or issued by an out-of-the-way publisher; who will always be prepared to advise you as to the latest work on any particular subject, as well as the best work.

These points are of greater importance to the live librarian than is the percentage of discount. Say nothing about per cents; to do so is misleading and unsatisfactory always. No one understands you.

It is safe to estimate that your purchases of fiction

and juvenile literature will average inside of $1 per volume

A general list, including reference books, of say 4000v., would average about $1.25 per volume, or $5000.

Make your purchases with the needs of your community clearly in mind, securing such books as will be constantly in use, and thereby get returns for your expenditure. The expensive publications and books that are called for only at rare intervals should be left to libraries with very large incomes, and to those making special collections.

Where possible to do so avoid buying large bills of books at long intervals. It is better to spend an income of $600 per year in monthly installments of $50, than it is to buy twice a year $300 lots.

The frequent purchase will bring you the new and talked of books while they are fresh in the minds of people, and there is greater economy of time in cataloging and shelving them.

Second-hand books are rarely cheap at any price.

Have confidence in your agent, for your interests are always his.

CHAPTER XVII

Ink and handwriting

For catalog cards and all other records use a non-copying black, permanent ink. Carter's record ink is good. It has been adopted, after careful investigation, by the state of Massachusetts for all official records. The New York state library school, at Albany, has issued a little handbook on "library handwriting," which recommends Carter's record, and says they use Stafford's blue writing ink for blue and his carmine combined for red.

For all labels on the outside of books, and for all writing on surfaces which may be much handled, use Higgins' American drawing ink, waterproof.

The vertical hand should be used in all library work. The following rules, with the illustrations, are taken from the Albany school handbook above referred to:

Brief rules.

1 **Ink.** Use only standard library ink and let it dry without blotting.

2 **Position.** Sit squarely at the desk and as nearly erect as possible.

3 **Alphabets.** Follow the library hand forms of all letters, avoiding any ornament, flourish, or lines not essential to the letter.

4 **Size.** Small letters, taking m as the unit, are one space or two millimeters high; i. e. one-third the distance between the rulings of the standard catalog card.

Capitals and extended letters are two spaces high above the base line or run one space below, except t, the character &, and figures, which are one and one-half spaces high.

5 Slant. Make letters upright with as little slant as possible, and uniformly the same, preferring a trifle backward rather than forward slant.

6 Spacing. Separate words by space of one m and sentences by two m's. Leave uniform space between letters of a word.

7 Shading. Make a uniform black line with no shading. Avoid hair line strokes.

8 Uniformity. Take great pains to have all writing uniform in size, slant, spacing, blackness of lines and forms of letters.

9 Special letters and figures. In both joined and disjoined hands dot i and cross t accurately to avoid confusion; e. g. Giulio carelessly dotted has been arranged under Guilio in the catalog. Cross t one space from line. Dot i and j one and one-half spaces from line. In foreign languages special care is essential.

Joined hand. Connect all the letters of a word into a single word picture. Complete each letter; e. g. do not leave gap between body and stem of b and d, bring loop of f back to stem, etc.

Avoid slanting r and s differently from other letters. They should be a trifle over one space in height. The small p is made as in print, and is not extended above the line as in ordinary script.

Disjoined hand. Avoid all unnecessary curves. The principal down strokes in b, d, f, h, i, j, k, l, m, n, p, q, r, t, u, and the first line in e, should be straight.

SPECIMEN ALPHABETS AND FIGURES

Joined Hand

a B c D Ɛ F G H I J K L
M N O P Q R S T U V V W
W X Y Y Z

a b c d e f f ß g g h h i j k k
l m n o p q r s b t u v w x y y
z

1 2 3 4 5 6 7 8 9 0 &

Take great pains to have all writing uniform in size, slant, spacing & forms of letters.

Disjoined Hand

A B C D E F G H I J K L M N
O P Q R S T U V W X Y Z

a b c d e f g h i j k l m n o p
q r s t u v w x y z

1 2 3 4 5 6 7 8 9 0 &

Take great pains to have all writing uniform in size, slant, spacing & forms of letters.

Make all the small letters, except f, i, j, k, t, x and y, without lifting pen from paper.

Make g and Q in one stroke, moving from left to right like the hands of a watch. Begin on the line.

Take special pains with the letter r, as carelessly made it is easily mistaken for v or y.

Make the upper part of B, R, and S a trifle smaller than the lower part.

Figures. Make all figures without lifting the pen. Begin 4 with the horizontal line. Make the upper part of 3 and 8 smaller than the lower part; 8 is best made by beginning in the center.

CHAPTER XVIII

The care of books

Books of moderate size should stand up on the shelves. Large books keep better if they are laid on their sides; when they stand, the weight of the leaves is a pull on the binding which tends to draw the books out of shape, and sometimes breaks them. Books which stand up should never be permitted to lean over, but should be kept always perfectly erect; the leaning wrenches them out of shape, and soon breaks the binding. A row of books which does not comfortably fill a shelf should be kept up at one end by a book support.

L. B. book supports. (Reduced.)

There are several good supports on the market. The Crocker is excellent; so is the one described in the Library Bureau catalog.

Books as they come from the dealer are not always perfect. To make sure that their purchases are in good condition some libraries collate all their books as soon as received, that is, look them through with care for missing pages, and injuries of any kind. Imperfect volumes are returned. But save with very expensive books this labor is unnecessary, and doesn't pay. The time spent on it easily amounts to more than the cost of replacing the very few books which may by chance be later found imperfect. In fact, any responsible dealer will usually replace an imperfect copy with a good one even if the former bears a library mark, and has been handled a little.

Use care in cutting pages. Don't cut them with anything but a smooth, dull edge. Cut them at the top close to the fold in the back.

The worst enemies of books are careless people.

Another enemy is damp. It is bad for the binding; it is very bad for the paper.

Gas, with heat, is very destructive to books, especially to the bindings.

Books should occasionally be taken from their shelves and wiped with a soft cloth. The shelves should at the same time be taken down and cleaned thoroughly.

Don't hold a book by one of its covers.

Don't pile up books very high.

Don't rub dust into them instead of rubbing it off.

Don't wedge books tightly into the shelves.

Those who use a public library are all desirous that its books be clean and neat, and with a little encouragement will take pretty good care of them. There are exceptions, of course, and especially among the children. These must be looked after and reasoned with.

Don't cover your books. The brown paper cover is an insult to a good book, a reproach to every reader of it, an incentive to careless handling, and an expense without good return.

A few simple rules like the following can be brought in an unobtrusive way to the attention of those who use the library. Always be sure that the library sets a good example in its handling of books.

Keep books dry.

Do not handle them when the hands are moist; of course never when the hands are soiled.

Use them to read, and for nothing else.

Never mark in them.

Do not turn down their pages.

Do not lay them face downwards.

Do not strap them up tightly.

Never let them fall.

Open them gently.

The book you are reading will go to others. Pass it on to them neat and clean, hoping that they will do the same by you.

CHAPTER XIX
Accessioning books

A careful record should be made of all books received. Use for this purpose what is called an accession book. This is a blank book, ruled and lettered

Date 29 S '92					
ACCESSION F.T.	CLASS	BOOK	VOL.	AUTHOR	TITLE
7581	428	B88		Bunce, O.B.	Don't
758+90 82		Z713		Zola, E.	Soil
Su.15x83	973.1	F54	v.1	Fiske, J.	Discovery of Amer.
84	973.1	F54	v.2	"	"
85					

Accession book, left-hand page. (Reduced size.)

PLACE AND PUBLISHER	DATE	BINDING	SOURCE	COST	REMARKS
N.Y.	App	1885	pa.	Scribner	28	O.ind. no. 354
L	Vizetelly	1888	cl.	"	81	" " 355
B	Ho.M	1892c	"	"	2 97	
"	"	"	"	"		

Accession book, right-hand page. (Reduced size.)

and numbered especially for library invoices. (See the Library Bureau catalog.) It is the library's chief record, and should contain a complete history of every volume on its shelves. The items entered in the accession book concerning every volume in the library are commonly the following: date of entry; accession number; class number (religion, sociology, etc.); author; title; place of publication and name of publisher; date of publication; binding (cloth, leather, etc.); size (octavo, quarto, etc.); number of pages; name of dealer from whom purchased; cost; remarks (maps, plates, etc.; books rebound; magazines, etc.; lost, worn out, replaced by another book, etc.).

Each book and each volume of a set has a separate accession number and a separate entry. Each entry occupies a line; each line is numbered from one up to such a number as the library has volumes. The number of each line, called the accession number, is written on the first page after the title-page of the book described on that line. The accession book is a life history of every book in the library. It forms such a record as any business-like person would wish to have of property entrusted to his care. It is also a catalog of all books in the library, and a useful catalog as long as the library is small. Never use an old accession number for a new book, even though the original book has disappeared from the library.

Record should be made of all books, pamphlets, reports, bulletins, magazines, etc., received by the library as gifts; and every gift should be promptly and courteously acknowledged in writing, even if previously acknowledged in person. Keep this record in a blank book, alphabetizing all gifts by the names of the givers, with dates of receipt. Books given should appear on the accession register the same as books purchased.

CHAPTER XX

Classifying books

The smallest public library should be classified and cataloged. This will make its resources more easily available, and will prevent the confusion and waste of labor which are sure to come if systematic treatment of the books is deferred. Get the best advice obtainable; consider the library's field and its possibilities of growth, and let the first work on the books be such as will never need to be done over.

To classify books is to place them in groups, each group including, as nearly as may be, all the books treating of a given subject, for instance, geology; or all the books, on whatever subject, cast in a particular form—for instance, poetry; or all the books having to do with a particular period of time—for instance, the middle ages. Few books are devoted exclusively to one subject and belong absolutely in any one class. The classification of books must be a continual compromise. Its purpose is not accurately to classify all printed things, this can't be done; but simply to make certain sources of information—books—more available. Any classification, if it gets the books on a given subject side by side, and those on allied subjects near one another, is a good one.

Books may be classified into groups in a catalog or list, yet themselves stand without order on the shelves. For convenience in getting for anyone all the books on a given subject, and especially for the help of those who are permitted to visit the shelves, all books should stand in their appropriate classes. Each book, therefore, should bear a mark which will tell in what class it belongs; distinguish it from all other books in that class; show where it stands on the shelves among its fellows of the same class; and indicate which one it is of several possible copies of the same book. This mark can be used to designate the book in all records of it, instead of the larger entry of its author and title.

There are two classification systems worthy of consideration, the Dewey, or decimal, and the Cutter, or expansive. They are outlined in the following chapters. Don't try to devise a system of your own.

Having decided on your system of classification, begin to classify. This is one of the many things which can only be learned by doing. Give fiction no class number, but an author number or "book-mark" only, as explained in a later chapter. Give all biography a single letter as its class number, and follow this by the author number.

Distinguish all juvenile books, whether fiction or other, by writing before their numbers some distinguishing symbol.

Take up first, in classification proper, the subjects of history and travel, which will be found comparatively easy.

It is easier to classify 25 or 50 books at a time in any given class than it is to classify them singly as you come to them in the midst of books of other classes. Consequently, group your books roughly into classes before you begin work on them.

As soon as a book is classified enter it at once in

your shelf-list—explained in a later chapter—and see that an author-card for it is put in the author catalog—explained later—with its proper number thereon.

If, after you have made up your mind, from an examination of the title-page, or table of contents, or a few pages here and there, what subject a book treats of in the main, you are still in doubt in what class to place it, consider what kind of readers will be likely to ask for it, and in what class they will be likely to look for it, and put it into that class. In doubtful cases the catalogs of other libraries are often good guides.

Keep your classification as consistent as possible. Before putting a book, about which there is any opportunity for choice, in the class you have selected for it, examine your shelf-list and see that the books already there are of like nature with it.

Classify as well as you can, and don't worry if you find you have made errors. There are always errors. Don't get into the habit of changing. Be consistent in classifying, and stick by what you have done.

CHAPTER XXI

The Dewey or Decimal system of classification

[From the Introduction to the Decimal classification and Relative index. Published by the Library Bureau, $5.]

The field of knowledge is divided into nine main classes, and these are numbered by the digits 1 to 9. Cyclopedias, periodicals, etc., so general in character as to belong to no one of these classes, are marked nought, and form a tenth class. Each class is similarly separated into nine divisions, general works belonging to no division having nought in place of the division number. Divisions are similarly divided into nine sections, and the process is repeated as often as necessary. Thus 512 means Class 5 (Natural science), Division 1 (Mathematics), Section 2 (Algebra), and every algebra is numbered 512.

The books on the shelves and the cards in the subject catalog are arranged in simple numerical order, all class numbers being decimals. Since each subject has a definite number, it follows that all books on any subject must stand together. The tables show the order in which subjects follow one another. Thus 512 Algebra precedes 513 Geometry, and follows 511 Arithmetic.

In the book after the tables of the classes arranged in their numerical order is an index, in which all the heads of the tables are arranged in one simple alphabet, with the class number of each referring to its exact place in the preceding tables. This index includes also, as far as they have been found, all the synonyms or alternative names for the heads, and many other entries that seem likely to help a reader find readily the subject sought. Though the user knows just where to turn to his subject in the tables, by first consulting the index he may be sent to other allied subjects, where he will find valuable matter which he would otherwise overlook.

The claims of the system may be summed up as follows: compared with other systems it is less expensive; more easily understood, remembered, and used; practical rather than theoretical; brief and familiar in its nomenclature; best for arranging pamphlets, sale duplicates, and notes, and for indexing; susceptible of partial and gradual adoption without confusion; more convenient in keeping statistics and checks for books off the shelves; the most satisfactory adaptation of the card catalog principle to the shelves. It requires less space to shelve the books; uses simpler symbols and fewer of them; can be expanded, without limit and without confusion or waste of labor, in both catalogs and on shelves, or in catalogs alone; checks more thoroughly and conveniently against mistakes; admits more readily numerous cross references; is unchangeable in its call-numbers, and so gives them in all places where needed, as given in no other system; in its index affords an answer to the greatest objection to class catalogs, and is the first satisfactory union of the advantages of the class and dictionary systems.

The Decimal system is used by a large number of libraries in this country, and has gained recognition and has been put to use by some librarians and men of science in Europe.

Divisions

000 General Works
- 010 Bibliography.
- 020 Library Economy.
- 030 General Cyclopedias.
- 040 General Collections.
- 050 General Periodicals.
- 060 General Societies.
- 070 Newspapers.
- 080 Special Libraries. Polygraphy.
- 090 Book Rarities.

100 Philosophy
- 110 Metaphysics.
- 120 Special Metaphysical Topics.
- 130 Mind and Body.
- 140 Philosophical Systems.
- 150 Mental Faculties. Psychology.
- 160 Logic.
- 170 Ethics.
- 180 Ancient Philosophers.
- 190 Modern Philosophers.

200 Religion
- 210 Natural Theology.
- 220 Bible.
- 230 Doctrinal Theol. Dogmatics.
- 240 Devotional and Practical.
- 250 Homiletic. Pastoral. Parochial.
- 260 Church. Institutions. Work.
- 270 Religious History.
- 280 Christian Churches and Sects.
- 290 Non-Christian Religions.

300 Sociology
- 310 Statistics.
- 320 Political Science.
- 330 Political Economy.
- 340 Law.
- 350 Administration.
- 360 Associations and Institutions.
- 370 Education.
- 380 Commerce and Communication
- 390 Customs. Costumes. Folk-lore.

400 Philology
- 410 Comparative.
- 420 English.
- 430 German.
- 440 French.
- 450 Italian.
- 460 Spanish.
- 470 Latin.
- 480 Greek.
- 490 Minor Languages.

500 Natural Science
- 510 Mathematics.
- 520 Astronomy.
- 530 Physics.
- 540 Chemistry.
- 550 Geology.
- 560 Paleontology.
- 570 Biology.
- 580 Botany.
- 590 Zoölogy.

600 Useful Arts
- 610 Medicine.
- 620 Engineering.
- 630 Agriculture.
- 640 Domestic Economy.
- 650 Communication and Commerce
- 660 Chemical Technology.
- 670 Manufactures.
- 680 Mechanic Trades.
- 690 Building.

700 Fine Arts
- 710 Landscape Gardening.
- 720 Architecture.
- 730 Sculpture.
- 740 Drawing, Design, Decoration.
- 750 Painting.
- 760 Engraving.
- 770 Photography.
- 780 Music.
- 790 Amusements.

800 Literature
- 810 American.
- 820 English.
- 830 German.
- 840 French.
- 850 Italian.
- 860 Spanish.
- 870 Latin.
- 880 Greek.
- 890 Minor Languages.

900 History
- 910 Geography and Description.
- 920 Biography.
- 930 Ancient History.
- 940 ⎧ Europe.
- 950 ⎪ Asia.
- 960 Modern ⎨ Africa.
- 970 ⎪ North America.
- 980 ⎪ South America.
- 990 ⎩ Oceanica and Polar Regions.

CHAPTER XXII

The Expansive classification: C. A. Cutter's

The classification

Those who have used it call it common-sense and up-to-date. They say that it is clear and easy to apply, and that it gives a suitable place for many classes of books for which other systems make no provision, or provide badly. It has been maturing for 20 years. Before it was printed it was applied (with a different notation) to the arrangement of a library of over 150,000 v. The experience thus gained has been supplemented as each part was prepared for the press by searching catalogs, bibliographies, and treatises on the subject classified. This ensured fullness. Overclassification, on the other hand, has been guarded against in four ways: 1) By not introducing at all distinctions that are purely theoretical or very difficult to apply; 2) by printing in small type those divisions which are worth making only when a large number of books calls for much subdivision; 3) by warning classifiers in the notes that certain divisions are needed only in large libraries; 4) by printing separately seven classifications of progressive fullness, the first having only 11 classes, which would be enough for a very small library; the second having 15 classes and 16 geographical divisions, suiting the small library when it has grown a little larger; the third having 30 classes and 29 geographical divisions; and so on, till the seventh would suffice for the very largest library. The same notation is used throughout, so that a library can adopt the fuller classification with the least possible change of mark.

It often suggests alternative places for a subject, stating the reasons for and against each, so that classifiers have a liberty of choice according to the character of their libraries, or of their clientage, or their own preferences.

The notation

The original feature of this notation is the use of letters to mark non-local subjects and figures for places. This makes it possible to express the local relations of a subject in a perfectly unmistakable way, the letters never being used to signify countries, and the figures never being used for any other subjects but countries. Thus 45 is England wherever it occurs; e. g. F being history and G geography, F45 is the history of England, G45 the geography of England. This local notation can be used not merely with the main classes, but in every subdivision, no matter how minute, which is worth dividing by countries. Whenever one wishes to separate what relates to England from other works on any subject one has only to add the two figures 45. Whenever one sees 45 in the mark of a book one knows that the book so marked treats its subject with special reference to England. This "local list" by the figures from 11 to 99 gives marks to the 88 most important countries. The addition of a third and sometimes of a fourth figure gives marks for all the independent countries in the world. Parts of and places in countries are arranged alphabetically under each, and are marked either by the usual Cutter order-table, which has initial letters followed by figures, or by a special Cutter order-table composed of figures alone.

Non-local subjects are marked with letters, first, to distinguish them from local subjects; and, second, because of the greater capacity. There are 26 main classes, A to Z. By adding a second letter these are divided into 676 parts, and these, by adding a third letter, into 17,576 parts, making 18,278 in all, so that as one uses successively three, four, or five characters, one gets respectively 18 times, 46 times, and 118 times the capacity of a decimal notation. The result is, short marks, numerous subdivisions, much greater elasticity, much greater power to properly express the relations of subjects to one another, and their relations to subordinate subjects, and much more opportunity of making the different portions of the classification correspond to each other.

The first part of the classification, as published, contains the first six classifications and a combined index to them all. The seventh, the fullest classification, will have 10 sections. Five of them are published, each with its own index. Of two (Social sciences and Language and literature) about half is published. When these and the other three (Natural sciences, Industrial arts, Recreative and fine arts) are printed, a full index to the whole will be made.

Expansive classification. Outline

A	**Generalia.**
A	General works.
Ae	General encyclopedias.
Ap	General periodicals.
Ar	Reference works.
As	General societies.

B–D   Spiritual sciences.

B	Philosophy.
Ba-Bf	National Philosophies and Systems of philosophy.
Bg	Metaphysics.
Bh	Logic.
Bi	Psychology.
Bm	Moral Philosophy.
Br	Religion, Natural theology.
Bt	Religions
Bu	Folk-lore.
Ca	Judaism.
Cb	Bible.
Cc	Christianity.
Cce	Patristics.
Ce	Apologetics, Evidences.
Cf	Doctrinal theology.
Ck	Ethical theology.
Cp	Ritual theology and church Polity.
Cx	Pastoral theology.
Cz	Sermons.
D	Ecclesiastical history.
Dk	Particular churches and sects.

E–G   Historical sciences.

E	Biography and Portraits.
F-Fz	History.
F	Universal history.
F02	Ancient history.
F03	Modern history.
F04	Medieval history.
F11-F99	History of single countries (using local list).
Fa-Fw	Allied studies, as Chronology, Philosophy of history, History of Civilization, Antiquities, Numismatics, Chivalry, Heraldry.
G	Geography, Travels.
G11-G99	Single countries (using local list).
Ga	Ancient geography.
Gf	Surveying and Map-making.
Gz	Maps.

H	**Social sciences.**
Hb	Statistics.
Hc	Economics.
He	Production.
Hf	Labor.
Hi	Slavery.
Hj	Transportation.
Hk	Commerce.
Hm	Money.
Hn	Banking.
Hr	Private finance.
Ht	Taxation and Public finance.
Hu	Tariff.
Hw	Property, Capital.
Hz	Consumption.
I	Demotics, Sociology.
Ic	Crime.
Ig	Charity.
Ih	Providence.
Ik	Education.
J	**Civics, Government, Political science.**
Ju	Constitutions and Politics.
K	**Law and Legislation.**
Kd	Public documents.
L-Q	**Natural sciences.**
L	General works, Metrics.
	L Number and space.
Lb	Mathematics.
	Lh-Lr Matter and force.
Lh	Physics.
Lo	Chemistry.
Lr	Astronomy.
	M-Q Matter and life.
M	Natural history.

Mg	Geology, incl. Mineralogy, Crystallography, Physical geography, Meteorology, Paleontology.
My	Biology.
N	Botany.
	Cryptogams.
	Phanerogams.
O	Zoology.
	Invertebrates.
P	Vertebrates.
Pg	Mammals.
Pw	Anthropology, Ethnology, Ethnography.
Q	Medicine.
Q-Z	**Arts.**
R	General works, Exhibitions, Patents.
Rd-Rg	Extractive arts.
Rd	Mining.
Re	Metallurgy.
Rf	Agriculture.
Rh	Horticulture.
Ri	Silviculture.
Rj	Animaliculture.
Rq	Chemic arts.
Rt	Electric arts.
Ry	Domestic arts.
Rz	Food and Cookery.
S	Constructive arts, Engineering.
Sg	Building.
Sj	Sanitary engineering.
Sl	Hydraulic engineering.
St	Transportation and Communication.
T	Fabricative arts, Machinery, Manufactures, and Handicrafts.
U	Protective arts, i. e., Military and Naval arts, Life-preserving, Fire fighting.

V	Athletic and Recreative arts, Sports and Games.
Vs	Gymnastics.
Vt	Theater.
Vv	Music.
W	Fine arts, plastic and graphic.
We	Landscape gardening.
Wf	Architecture.
Wj	Sculpture.
Wk	Casting, Baking, Firing.
Wm	Drawing.
Wp	Painting.
Wq	Engraving.
Wr	Photography.
Ws	Decorative arts, including Costume.
X-Yf	Communicative arts (by language).
X	Philology.
X	Inscriptions.
X	Language.
Y	Literature.
Yf	English Fiction.
Z	Book arts (making and use of books).
Za-Zk	Production.
Za	Authorship.
Zb	Rhetoric.
Zd	Writing.
Zh	Printing.
Zk	Binding.
Zl	Distribution (Publishing and Bookselling).
Zp	Storage and Use (Libraries).
Zt	Description (Zt Bibliography; Zx Selection of reading; Zy Literary history; Zz National bibliography.)

CHAPTER XXIII

Author-numbers, or book-marks

The books in a given group or class should stand on the shelves in the alphabetical order of their authors' names, though this is not necessary in a small library. This result is best secured by adding to the class-mark of every book another mark, called an author-number or book-number or book-mark, made up of the first letter of the author's name and certain figures. Books bearing these author-numbers, if arranged first alphabetically by the letters, and then in the numerical order of the numbers following the letters, will always stand in the alphabetical order of the authors' names. Different books by the same author are distinguished from one another by adding other figures to the author-number, or by adding to the author-numbers the first letter of the title of each book.

These book-marks cannot be chosen arbitrarily. They should be taken from the printed set of them worked out by Mr Cutter, and called the Cutter author-tables. (See Library Bureau catalog.)

In a very small library the books in a given class can be distinguished one from another by writing after the class-number of each book the number of that book in its class. If the class-mark of religion, for example, is 20, the books successively placed in that class will bear the numbers 20.1, 20.2, 20.3, etc.

Fiction should have author-numbers only. The absence of a class-number will sufficiently distinguish it from other classes.

CHAPTER XXIV

The shelf-list

Many books can be very properly put in any one of several different classes. In which one a given book should be placed will often be decided by noting where other like books have been placed. Books by authors of the same name will often fall into the same class, and to each of these a different author-number

Shelf list sheet. (Reduced; actual size, 10 x 25 cm.)

must be given. You must have at hand, then, a list of the books already classified, to see at once, in classifying the next book, what kinds of books and books by what authors are in each class. Every book in the library, as soon as it has been classified, and has received its proper author-number, should be entered in a list in the order first of its class-number, next of its author-number. This list is called the shelf-list. It is commonly kept on sheets, but many librarians believe it best kept on cards; a card for each different book. It is a catalog of all the books in the library arranged in the order in which they stand on the shelves. It is a subject-index of the library. It is indispensable in the work of properly placing, class-numbering, and author-numbering new books. It is a list from which it is very easy to check over the library and learn what books are missing or out of place. It includes usually only the class- and author-number, author's name, brief title, and accession number. This last enables one to refer at once from the brief entry of a certain book in the shelf-list to the full information in the accession book.

090	Slater	
S11		Book collecting
		3528

Shelf-list card. (Reduced; actual size, 5 x 12½ cm.)

There are advantages in adding to the shelf-list record the publisher and price. As soon as a book has received its class- and author-numbers, which together are sometimes called the "call-number," as being the mark to be used by the public in calling for a book, these numbers, or combinations of numbers and letters, should be written in the accession book in a column left for the purpose, on the line given up to the description of the book in hand. This enables one to refer at once from the accession entry of a given book to the shelf-list entry of the same book.

CHAPTER XXV

Cataloging books

After the books are accessioned, classified, author-numbered or book-marked, and shelf-listed, they should be cataloged. A catalog is a labor-saving device in library work. From it both reader and attendant can ascertain whether the library has a certain book. By consulting the catalog for the class-number, the book may be looked for in its proper place, thus often saving hunting through the shelves in several classes.

A printed list or catalog of the library is one of the first things that will be asked for by the public. It is useful especially for those who cannot well visit the library. But it is very expensive; it is out of date as soon as issued; it cannot often be sold; it requires training and experience to make it properly, and the money it will cost can be better spent otherwise. Do not issue one. Print lists of additions in newspapers. Post them in the library. Issue an occasional bulletin of the latest purchases if you think it will be popular. Put your time, skill, energy, and money into the making of a full card catalog; keep this up to date; give the public access to it; teach them how to use it, and you will find the printed catalog not needed.

On cards prepared for the purpose [see chapter on Things needed (9) and Library Bureau catalog], a card for each book—and a book is a book although in several volumes—write the author's surname (if the book is anonymous write first the title), given name or names, if known, title, date of copyright, date of publication, call-number, and such other data as seem desirable. The price, for example, may be put here, and the size, indicating this by a letter. [See Cole size card in chapter on Things needed (9) and in Library Bureau catalog.] Arrange these cards alphabetically, by authors' names for an author catalog. This catalog will be in constant use in the purchasing of books, in classifying new purchases, etc. By the call-number one can refer from any entry in it to the entry of the same book in the shelf-list. To make possible a like reference to the

3732	Coffin, Charles Carleton, 1823–
C 63	Old times in the colonies.
	460 p. il. O N.Y. [1880]

Author card. (Reduced; actual size, 7½ x 12½ cm.)

accession book, write the accession number of each book near the bottom of the card on which it is entered. In making the catalog entries observe certain fixed rules of alphabetization, capitalization, punctuation, arrangement, etc., as set forth in the catalog rules which may be adopted. Only by so doing can you secure uniformity of entry, neatness in work, and the greatest possible meaning from every note, however much abbreviated.

Preserve this catalog with great care. It is the key to the records in shelf-list and accession book. In a small library the public may very properly use it. As soon as possible, if your library is to be quite large and much used, prepare for public use a duplicate of it, omitting all those entries in the original which are of use only to the librarian.

The average reader more often remembers the titles of books than their authors. Add, therefore, to the author-list, in your public catalog—not in your private or official catalog, for which author-entries alone are sufficient—a title-list; a set of cards like the author cards, except that on each one the book's title is entered first instead of its author. Arrange author and title-lists in one alphabetical series.

973.2	Old times in the colonies
C65	Coffin, C.C.

Title card. (Reduced; actual size, 7½ x 12½ cm.)

As the use of the library for reference work increases, the question will often be asked, has it any books on a certain subject? Add, therefore, to your author- and title-list a subject-list. Make this by writing a card for each book with the subject of which it treats the first word upon it. Arrange this also in the same alphabetical series with the other two. In some cases the book's title and its subject will be identical; for example, Geology, by Tompkins, or Washington's boyhood, by Jones. For such books one card answers for title and subject. For fiction no subject-card is necessary. On the other hand, many books have to do with more than one subject; a volume of essays, for example, or a group of biographical sketches. For such it is desirable to add to the subject-list by writing as many cards for each book as the importance of the several subjects therein and the space the author gives to them seem to demand. Each card will have for the first word of its entry the subject to which it refers, followed by the author and title of the book.

Arrange these cards also alphabetically with all the others. Put on every card in the catalog the call-number of the book to which it refers. This author-title-subject-list, or dictionary catalog, will tell at a glance if the library has books a) by a certain author; b) with a given title; c) on a given subject. These are the questions most often asked.

973.2	U.S. history — colonial
C65	Coffin, Charles Carleton, 1823–
	Old times in the colonies
	460 p. il. O N.Y. 1880.

Subject card. (Reduced; actual size, 7½ x 12½ cm.)

There are in print several books giving rules for cataloging. Some of these are mentioned in the chapter on Things needed (9). In a small library which is always to be small it is not necessary to follow all the rules laid down in these books. It is much better, however, to do all the work, even in a very small library, according to the most approved methods. So to do brings you in touch with your fellows and gives you the comfort which comes from the consciousness of work well done, even if the amount of the work be small.

In writing the subject-headings difficulties will soon arise unless you follow certain general rules and are careful also to be consistent in your work. For instance, at intervals during a few months you add to the library books on horses, cows, sheep, goats, camels, and pigs; some dealing with one animal, some with two or more. If for the first one you write a subject-card with the catch-word or entry-word at the top "Domestic animals," and for the next one "Farm animals," and for the next one "Animals, domestic," you will scatter the references to domesticated animals all through your catalog, to the despair of those who would use it. You can guard against this, and easily, if your catalog is small, by looking to see what you have already written every time you write a new subject-entry-word, and by following out a previously devised plan in the making of your entries. The safest way is to get a printed list of headings and catalog rules and follow them. (See chapter on Things needed, 9.)

With a printed list of subject-headings at hand it is not difficult to keep your catalog consistent and reasonable.

This same list of subject-headings will serve also as a guide in the writing of the cross-reference cards for your catalog, the cards, that is, which refer the searcher from the topic "pigs," for example, to "swine," or from both to "domestic animals."

Of course the subject-headings' list must be systematically used, and must be marked and annotated to fit your special needs. This work, like classifying, can best be learned by doing.

There are many ways of keeping your catalog cards. The thing to use is a set of trays made for the purpose. (See Library Bureau catalog.) The cards are extremely valuable, and expense should not be spared in providing for their safe keeping and handy use.

CHAPTER XXVI

Preparing books for the shelves

All books should be marked with the name of the library. This is cheaply done with a rubber stamp and violet or red ink pad. An embossing stamp makes a good and indelible mark. The type used should be of moderate size and open faced. A perforating stamp now on the market marks a book neatly and most permanently. Mark books freely, to assure their being

Embossing stamp.

recognized as the library's property wherever seen. Have some definite pages on which stamps always appear. Many use the title-page, fifty-first or one hundred and first, and the last page. This need not interfere with marking elsewhere.

On the back of the book write the call-number. For this purpose use a tag or label. They can be had in several sizes; round ones are best. Paste the label where it will mar the book least, as near the middle as possible. It is well to put all labels at the same height from the bottom of the back, so far as this can be done without covering essential parts of the lettering. Four inches is a good height for the lower edge of all labels. Labels stick better if the place where they are to be pasted is moistened with a solution of ammonia and water, to remove varnish or grease. If this is done the mucilage or gum on the labels when purchased will be found usually to stick well. After the call-number is written, varnish the label with a thin solution of shellac in alcohol. Labels put on in this way will keep clean, remain legible, and rarely come off.

If a charging system using a pocket is adopted, no book-plate is needed, if the pocket, that is, is pasted on the inside of the front cover and has the name of the library on it.

When books are classified the call-number is written with hard pencil on a certain page, the same page in all books; a common place is the first right hand page after the title-page, and near the inner margin.

This call-number should be written with ink on the pocket and book slip, which is kept in the pocket, or on the book-plate. It is advisable also to write the call-number in ink on some definite page bearing the library's stamp.

If a book-plate is adopted let it be small and simple. Have a special plate for gifts, with space on it for writing the name of the giver.

Books wear better if they are carefully opened in a number of places before they are placed on the shelves. This makes the backs flexible and less likely to break with rough handling. In cutting the leaves be sure that the paper knife does its work to the very back edge of the top folds, that it is never sharp enough to cut down into the leaves, and that it is held nearly parallel to the fold to be cut.

The following is a list of things to be done before books are ready for use in a public library:

1 Book notices and reviews are read and the library's needs and funds considered.

2 Order slips are made out, arranged alphabetically, and compared with the catalog to see if the books listed on them are already in the library.

3 Order list is made out, approved, and sent to dealer.

4 Books arrive and are checked by the bill, and brief notes of date of purchase, initials of dealer, and price are written on the left margin of the second page after the title-page.

5 Bill is checked for items and prices by order slips.

6 Gifts when received are a) properly acknowledged; b) entered in gift book; c) marked with small gift-book plates pasted inside the front cover.

7 Books are looked over (if you wish), collated, especially the expensive ones, to see if complete and sound.

8 Books are entered in the accession book.

9 Books are stamped with library stamp.

10 Books are opened to loosen binding, and pages cut, if necessary.

11 The book-plates are pasted inside the front cover—if book-plates are used.

12 Pockets are pasted on the inside of front cover or wherever the system adopted places them.

13 Labels are put on the backs.

14 Books are classified, author-numbered and call-numbered.

15 Books are entered on shelf-list.

16 Catalog cards are written—author, title, and subject.

17 Bulletin lists of the books are made out for posting up and for newspapers.

18 Call-numbers are written on the labels, the pockets, and the book slips.

19 Labels are varnished.

20 The call-number of each book is entered in the proper place on the line which that book occupies in the accession book.

21 Books are placed on the library shelves for public use.

22 Catalog cards, author, title, and subject, are arranged alphabetically in one series and distributed in catalog.

CHAPTER XXVII
Binding and mending

Binding a book means not only covering it, but preserving it. Good binding, even at a high price, educates the public taste and promotes a desire to protect the library from injury and loss. Cheap binding degrades books and costs more in the end than good work.

Keep in a bindery-book, which may be any simple blank book, or one especially made for the purpose (see Library Bureau catalog), a record of each volume that the library binds or rebinds.

Enter in the bindery-book consecutive bindery number, book-number, author, title, binding to be used, date sent to bindery, date returned from bindery, and cost of binding.

Books subject to much wear should be sewn on tapes, not on strings; should have cloth joints, tight backs, and a tough, flexible leather, or a good, smooth cloth of cotton or linen such as is now much used by good binders. Most of the expensive leather, and all cheap leather, rots in a short time; good cloth does not. Very few libraries can afford luxurious binding. Good material, strong sewing, and a moderate degree of skill and taste in finishing are all they can pay for. Learn to tell a substantial piece of work when you see it, and insist that you get such from your binder. The beginners' first business is to inform himself carefully as to character, value, cost and strength of all common binding materials.

From binders, or from dealers in binding material, you can get samples of cloth, leather, tapes, string, thread, etc., which will help you to learn what to ask for from your local binder.

The following notes are from a lecture by John H. H. McNamee before the Massachussets library club in 1896, on the Essentials of good binding:

"Had I the ordering of bindings for any public or circulating library where books are given out to all classes of people, and subjected to the handling which such books must receive, I should, from my experience as a binder, recommend the following rules:

For the smaller volumes of juveniles, novels, and perishable books (by which I mean books which are popular for a short time, and then may lie on the shelves almost as so much lumber), have each book pulled to pieces and sewed with Hayes' linen thread on narrow linen tapes, with edges carefully trimmed.

Have the books rounded and backed, but not laced in. Have the boards placed away from the backs about one-fourth of an inch, in order to give plenty of room for them to swing easily and avoid their pulling off the first and last signatures of the book when opened. Give the back and joint a lining of super or cheese cloth. Have them covered with American duck or canvas pasted directly to the leaves, pressed well and given plenty of time to dry under pressure, and so avoid as much as possible all warping of boards and shrinkage of the cloth. For all large folios, newspapers and kindred works, use heavy canvas, as it is somewhat cheaper than sheep, and as easily worked. Have them sewed strongly on the requisite number of bands, every band laced into the boards, which should be made by pasting two heavy binder's boards together, to prevent warping and give solidity to the volume.

The reason I say lace in large volumes is that the heavy books will sag and pull out of covers by their great weight unless tightly fastened to a solid board, thus giving the book a good foundation to stand on.

For all periodicals not bound in leather I should prescribe the same treatment. These volumes can be lettered in ink on the canvas, or in gold on a colored leather label pasted on the cloth. But for all books which are destined to be bound in leather I should surely, and without any hesitation whatever, order morocco, and by this I mean goat skin, and I should go still further and demand a good German or French goat; boards hard and laced in at every band, super joints, full, open backs, lettering clear and distinct, and the paper on the sides to match the leather.

I would also recommend that a schedule be used, giving a space for schedule number; then the name of book or books, or lettering to be used on each volume; space for the number of volumes, space for description of binding, and finally for price, thus giving the binder a complete order on a large sheet, which he is in no danger of losing. All he will have to do is to mark on the title of each volume, in small figures, its schedule number, and, when the books are done, put down the prices and add up the column of figures, and make out his statement as per the number of schedule.

This method gives the librarian a complete list of volumes sent and returned, and by laying away these schedules she has for handy reference a very complete list of prices. It saves the binder from writing out the name of each volume on his bill, and as the librarian must keep a list of books sent, why not keep them this way as well as any other? I have mislaid or lost hundreds of lettering slips, which are the bane of a bookbinder's existence. Lay down some rules for the cutting of books, placing of plates, binding of covers, and advertisements, style of lettering, etc., and have your binder follow them.

Don't ever cut with a folder before sending to binder, as it makes the sewing more difficult.

Don't pull to pieces or take out titles and indexes. The binder always takes care of that.

Don't take off ads, as it sometimes leaves unsightly tears or takes away pages, and if all leaves are paged the binder is at a loss to know if the book is complete.

Don't ever use mucilage or glue. Your bookbinder will send you a little paste, or you can make it by boiling flour and water and sprinkling in a little salt. If you wish to keep it for a long time, mix a few drops of oil of cloves with it and seal up.

Of course there are cases where some of these rules don't apply, such as volumes made up from leaves taken from several other volumes or pamphlets.

In case of a book of this kind place every leaf in correct order, and write directions very carefully."

Many books will need repair. A few hours spent in the bindery, studying the methods of putting a book together, will be helpful, not only in the matter of securing good binding, but in the repairing of books that have gone to pieces. Mend and rebind your books the minute they seem to need it. Delay is the extravagant thing in this case. If you are slow in this matter, leaves and sections will be lost, and the wear the broken-backed volume is getting will soon remove a part of the fold at the back of the several sections, and make the whole book a hopeless wreck forever.

CHAPTER XXVIII

Pamphlets

Save all pamphlets having to do with local history, and save also those of a general nature which promise ever to be of any importance. In a small library, however, or in any library in which money for salaries is limited, and the work to be done in the regular matter

L. B. pamphlet case. (Various sizes.)

of attending to the public, lending books, etc., is great, do not waste time in trying to arrange or catalog pamphlets. Simply let them accumulate, arranging them roughly in classes. Bind at once only those that seem absolutely to demand it. In the history of almost any library the time will come when it will be possible to sort out pamphlets, arrange them properly, catalog such as are worth it, bind them singly or in groups, and incorporate them into the library. But any system of arranging and sorting pamphlets which does anything more than very roughly to arrange and store them, and attempts to make them, without much labor, accessible to the general public, is almost sure to be a failure. This is not true of pamphlets to which the public has not access. But pamphlets not fully cataloged and not accessible to the public are, no matter how scientifically arranged, almost useless plunder. To keep them clean and in order nothing is as good as a pamphlet case, which any boxmaker can make, of cardboard about 9 inches high, 7 inches deep, and 2 inches thick, open at the back. They will cost from 4 to 12 cents each, according to quality of board used and quantity ordered. For holding a few pamphlets together temporarily Ballard's "klips" are best. Sold by H. H. Ballard, Pittsfield, Mass.

CHAPTER XXIX

Public documents

Adelaide R. Hasse, of the New York Public library

How issued

Government documents are issued in two sets or editions, viz.: the Congressional or sheep, and the Departmental or cloth. The annual reports of the heads of departments, with many of the serial and occasional publications of the various departments, are contained in the sheep set, and in addition, all the reports of committees, and records of the transactions of congress, except the debates which are contained in the Congressional record. The cloth set contains all the publications of the various departments, irrespective of the fact that some of them may have appeared in the sheep set.

To whom issued

The depository libraries receive the sheep set by law from the superintendent of documents. Each department has its own list of "exchanges" (i. e., designations) which receive gratis the publications of that department intended for general distribution. Non-depository libraries receive their documents regularly from the departments when on the department exchange list, or irregularly from their representatives in congress. "Remainder libraries" receive from the superintendent of documents such documents as can be supplied from the fractional quotas sent to him after the editions ordered for the use of congress have been equally divided among the senators and representatives.

"Special libraries" are those libraries specially designated by members of congress to receive the publications of the geological survey.

Many thousands of books have been sent on special application to libraries not on the list. The depository, remainder, and special libraries together now number over 1300.

All the departments still control the distribution of their own publications, the superintendent of documents only distributing the sheep set, and such of the department publications as have been turned over to him by the departments for this purpose, or of which there have been remainders. Sometimes the number of copies of its own publications allotted to the department is very small and soon exhausted.

Librarians and others who want full information about the distribution, present methods of issue, etc., of public documents, should send for the First annual report of the superintendent of documents. In addition there have been issued from his office, since its establishment in March, 1895, a check list of public documents, and since January, 1895, a monthly catalog of current publications. Both are mailed free upon application.

Care in a library

The question of the most economical, and at the same time satisfactory manner of caring for documents in a library, cannot be considered in the space of so brief an article as this necessarily must be. After all, it is a question that must be settled by each library for itself, since it rests chiefly upon the extent to which the library can afford duplication.

Depository libraries have better opportunities than

others for filling up the sheep set, and having this set they have the greater portion of those documents useful to the average library. A complete sheep set from the 15th Congress to the close of the 53d Congress numbers slightly over 3343v., and will require 860 feet of shelving, or six modern iron book stacks.

Though it is done in a few cases, the subject classification of the sheep set is not to be recommended. Where subject classification, or the incorporation of the documents in the general library, is desired, the cloth set is preferable, and is in most cases procurable. If a library can afford shelf room for both, it will be found more satisfactory to keep the sheep set intact, and to make a selection of such reports from the cloth set as will be locally useful to the library.

No small library should undertake to acquire any documents but those for which it has an actual use; only the largest libraries can afford the task of filling up sets of documents simply for the sake of having a complete record.

Small libraries, and all libraries in need of any special report or document, can get it, in most cases, by applying to the superintendent of documents. Return all your duplicates to the superintendent of documents; arrangements for their transportation will be made by him upon notification, and anything he has that is needed will be sent in exchange.

Do not try to collect a complete set of government documents; the government of the United States has not yet been able to do that.

CHAPTER XXX
Checking the library

Check the library over occasionally. It need not be done every year. It is an expensive thing to do, in time, and is not of great value when done; but now and then it must be gone through with. It is not necessary to close the library for this purpose. Take one department at a time and check it by the shelf-list. Make a careful list of all books missing. Check this list by the charging slips at the counter. For those still missing make a general but hasty search through the library. Go over each part of the library in this way. Then compile all lists of missing books into one list, arranged in the order of their call-numbers. Once or twice a week for several months go over the library with this list, looking for missing books. Even with access to the shelves, and with great freedom in matters of circulation, not many books will be found missing, under ordinary circumstances, at the end of a six months' search. Such books as are still missing at the end of any given period, together with those that have been discarded as worn out, and those that have been lost by borrowers, should be properly marked on the shelf-list, and should have an entry in the accession book, stating what has become of them. If they are not replaced, it will be advisable to withdraw the cards representing them from the card catalog, or to write on the cards the fact of withdrawal and the cause.

Keep a record of all books withdrawn from the library for whatever reason.

CHAPTER XXXI

Lists, bulletins, printed catalog

Give the public access to the card catalog if possible. If a dictionary catalog is made it will prove to be most helpful to the serious students. For the average reader, the person who wishes to get a recent book, the latest novel, etc., prepare lists of additions from month to month, post them up in some convenient place in the library, and put them in a binder to be left on desk or table in the delivery room.

Print lists of additions, if possible, in the local papers; also publish reference lists having to do with current events and matters of popular interest. Oftentimes the newspapers will furnish, for a small sum, extra copies of the lists which they have printed. If the means warrant the expenditure, a periodical bulletin, appearing once a month, or even oftener, containing information about the library, notes on recent additions, suggestions as to the use of books, lists on special subjects, and lists of books lately added may prove useful. Such a bulletin can often be maintained without cost to the library by having it published by some one who will pay its expenses by means of advertisements. The very best way of bringing new books to the attention of readers is to print a list of additions, with call-numbers, as condensed as possible, and with no other matter, for free distribution in the library.

In printing lists of books, make the classes covered special, not general. Give lists suitable for as many different needs and occasions as possible. There can't be too many of them. For instance, a teacher would find thoroughly helpful and practicable such classified lists of books as, for beginners in third and fourth grades, for the intermediate pupils, for boys, for girls, numerous references to the current events of the day; historical readings divided into periods and adapted to different grades; historical fiction under several forms of classification; biographies and biographical sketches suited to different ages; geographical aids, including travel, description, life, scenes, and customs in different countries; natural history and elementary science; the resources of the library available for the purpose of illustrating topics in history, art, and science; material for theme studies; special lists for anniversary days now so generally observed in schools, and so on.

Lists in which the titles of the books come first are better liked by the general public than are author-lists. People commonly know books by name, not by author.

Don't make the mistake of spending much money, at the library's beginning, for a printed catalog. A printed catalog, as stated in chapter 25, is not a necessity. It is useful, particularly for home use, to tell whether the library owns certain books; but with a good card catalog, newspaper lists, special lists, and the like, it is not a necessity. Few large libraries now publish complete catalogs.

CHAPTER XXXII

Charging system

On the inside of the front cover of every book in the library paste a manilla pocket. (See Library Bureau catalog.) Or paste, by the bottom and the upper corners, thus making a pocket of it, a sheet of plain, stout paper at the bottom of the first page of the first flyleaf. On this pocket, at the top, write the call-number of the book. Below this print information for borrowers, if this seems necessary. In this pocket place a book-card of heavy ledger paper or light cardboard. On this book-card, at the top, write the call-number of the book in the pocket of which it is placed.

To every borrower the library issues a borrower's card. This card is made of heavy, colored tag-board, and contains the borrowers'

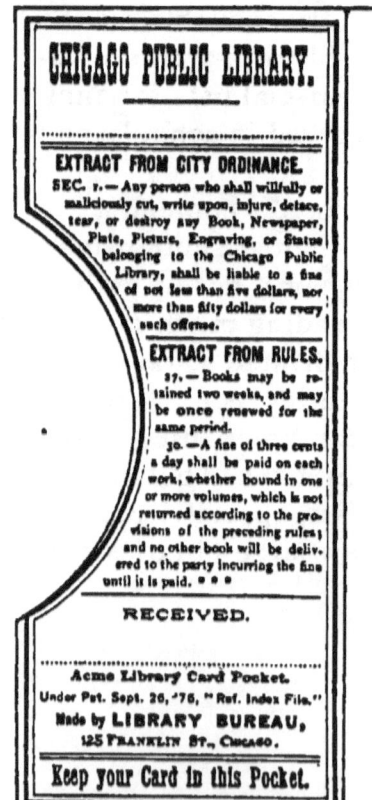

Card-pocket.
(Reduced; actual size, 7x13½ cm.)

name and address, and his number in the series of borrowers' numbers.

The librarian, before delivering a book to a borrower, takes from the pocket the book-card, writes on it the number found at the top of the borrower's card, and after it, with a dater, stamps the day of the month. At the same time he stamps the same date on the borrower's card, and on the pocket in the book or on a dating slip pasted in the book opposite the pocket.

The borrower's card he places in the book pocket, the book-card he retains as a record of the loan, and the borrower takes the book away. The book-card, with all others representing the books issued on the same day, he places in a tray behind a card bearing the date of the day of issue. All the book-cards representing books issued on

Book card.
(Reduced; actual size, 12½x7½cm.)

Tray for book-cards.

a certain day are arranged in the order of their call-numbers.

Under this system the borrower can tell, by looking at his card, on what date the book he has was taken from the library. If he wishes to renew it without taking it back to the library, he can do so by a letter stating that he took on a certain day a book bearing a certain number, and wishes it renewed.

The librarian can tell, from the book-cards, what books are in circulation, and how many of each class were lent on a certain day.

City Library Association.

Springfield, Mass. _Feb. 14, 1899_

The book noted below is now in the library and will be reserved for you until 9 P. M., _Feb. 15._

Please present this notice and your library card. A charge of two cents is made for this notice.

JOHN COTTON DANA, *Librarian.*

Book No. _2173.54_   Per _S.m.J._

Title, etc. _Ave Roma Immortalis_

Reserve Postal Form 1 Jan. 30, '48. 5m.

No. 1. Postal notice. (Reduced.)

The borrower's number, written on the book-card of any given book in circulation, will give, through the register of borrowers, the name and address of the person having that book. Overdue books are automatically indicated, their cards remaining in the tray, behind the card indicating the date they were lent, after the day for their return has passed.

When a borrower returns a book the librarian can learn, from the date on the pocket, whether or no a fine should be paid on it; if not, he can, if in haste, immediately take out the borrower's card from the

```
┌─────────────────────────────────────────────────┐
│ Name,  Geo. Brown,              No. 80          │
│                                                 │
│ Residence,  72 Vernon.                          │
│                                                 │
│                                                 │
│ Employment,  Machinist,                         │
│                                                 │
│ Employer,  Smith & Wesson's.                    │
│                                                 │
│ Place of business,  85 Main.                    │
│                                                 │
│  No. OK  11-05-5M.                              │
└─────────────────────────────────────────────────┘
```

No. 2. Registration card, face. (Reduced; actual size, 7½ x 12½ cm.)

book pocket, stamp the date of its return at the right of the date on which it was lent, thus canceling the

```
┌─────────────────────────────────────────────────┐
│                             Feb. 14, 1899.      │
│    I hereby declare that I am a resident of the City of Springfield, and in │
│  consideration of the right to use the Free City Library, agree to comply with │
│  all Regulations provided for its government.  │
│                                                 │
│              George Brown.                      │
│                                                 │
│    I hereby certify that the above subscriber is a fit person to enjoy the │
│  privileges of the City Library, and that I will be responsible for any loss or in- │
│  jury the Library may sustain from the permission given to draw books in con- │
│  sequence of this certificate.                  │
│                                                 │
│  Signature (in ink)                             │
│                                                 │
│  Residing at No.                      Street.   │
└─────────────────────────────────────────────────┘
```

No. 3. Registration card, reverse. (Reduced; actual size, 7½ x 12½ cm.)

charge against the borrower, and lay the book aside and look up its book-card later.

Double and special borrowers' cards are not needed under this system. It accommodates itself readily to a "two-book" system. On the book-cards belonging to the second book, and all other books after the first, which any borrower may take, the librarian writes the borrower's number preceded by any letter or sign which will serve to indicate that these books are charged, not on the borrower's card, but to the borrower direct, on

---

The City Library Association, Springfield, Mass.
LITERATURE: ART: SCIENCE.

The Library: Circulating Department.

The rules of the library require all books to be returned in two weeks. Book No. G 647.2 stands charged to you (Card No. 1906) as taken from the library Feb. 2 '99. You are incurring a fine of two cents for every day's detention. If you think a mistake has been made, please notify us.
A charge of two cents is made for sending this notice.

The City Library.
Per B.

No. 87 11—98—n   **Present this notice with your library card.**

No. 4. Overdue notice. (Postal card, reduced.)

the strength of a general permission to him to take more than one book.

The postal notice no. 1, the registration cards 2 and 3, the notice that the book is overdue, no. 4, the fine slip, no. 5, all explain themselves.

In most places, certainly in all small towns, a sufficient safeguard against the loss of books is found in the signature of the borrower himself. No guarantee need be called for. To ask for a guarantor for a reputable resident is simply to discommode two people instead of one. The application which the borrower signs should be brief and plain. Name, residence, place of business, and any necessary references, should be written in by the librarian on one side; the signature to an agreement to obey the library rules can be written by the applicant on the other. All borrowers' agreements should be filed in alphabetical order. They should receive borrowers' numbers in the order of their issue, and the date. The borrowers' cards should state that they expire in a definite number of years from the date of issue, and the date of issue should be stamped on them. An index of borrower's agreements should be kept by their numbers. This need contain only the borrower's number, his name, and, when necessary, his address. It is conveniently kept in a book. It is better to keep it on cards.

No. 5. Fine slip.
(Reduced; actual size 12½x7½cm.)

CHAPTER XXXIII

Meeting the public

If the public is not admitted to the shelves, it will be necessary to supply catalogs for public use as well as slips on which lists of books wanted can be made out; but the fullest possible catalogs and the finest appointments in the delivery room cannot take the place of direct contact between librarian or assistants and the public. Wherever possible, the person to whom the borrower applies for a book should go himself to the shelves for it.

The stranger in the library should be made welcome. Encourage the timid, volunteer to them directions and suggestions, and instruct them in the library's methods. Conversation at the counter having to do with wants of borrowers should be encouraged rather than discouraged. No mechanical devices can take the place of face to face question and answer.

The public like to handle and examine their books, and it is good for them to do it. They like the arrangements in the library to be simple; they object to red tape and rules. They like to have their institutions seem to assume—through, for example, the absence of signs—that they know how to conduct themselves courteously without being told. They don't like delays. They like to be encouraged to ask questions. They like to be consulted as to their wants, and as to changes in arrangements and methods. They like to feel at home in their library.

CHAPTER XXXIV

The public library for the public

The librarian of former times was almost invariably a bookworm, and was often a student properly so called. The older librarians of the present day, and the librarians of the great libraries of our cities, are also very commonly men of letters, men of learning, men who admire the student spirit and know how to appreciate it. The librarian of former days actually felt that the books of which he had charge were to be used, if they were used at all, chiefly, if not only, by persons who wished to make some careful and painstaking research; and the older librarians, and the librarians of the greater libraries of today, are also inclined to think that their libraries are best used, or at least are used as fully as they need be, when they are visited by those who are engaged in original investigation or serious study of some sort. As a fellow librarian once wrote me, for example, of one of his colleagues, "His whole trend is scholarly rather than popular; he appreciates genuine contributions to art, science, and industry, but has little taste for the great class of books that the main body of readers care for." This view of literature, libraries, and the use of books, and this special fondness for what may be called genuine contributions to art, science, and industry, are proper enough in their time and place; but it cannot be too often impressed upon the library world, and upon those who contribute to the support of libraries, and upon trustees and directors generally, that the thing that is of great consequence in the work of the free public library is not its product in the shape of books which are the results of careful research, or of books which are contributions to science, art, and industry; it is the work that the library does from day to day in stimulating the inquiring spirit, in adding to the interest in things, and in broadening the minds of the common people who form 90 per cent at least of the public library patrons. That is to say, the public library is chiefly concerned not in the products of education, as shown in the finished book, but in the process of education as shown in the developing and training of the library users, of the general public.

It is from this common-folks-education point of view that the advocate of the open-shelf system looks upon the question of library administration. A free public library is not a people's post-graduate school, it is the people's common school.

The more I see and learn of free public libraries the more I am convinced that a public library can reach a high degree of efficiency in its work only when its books are accessible to all its patrons. The free public library should not be managed for the use of the special student, save in special cases, any more than is the free public school. That it should be solely or chiefly or primarily the student's library, in any proper sense of the word, is as contrary to the spirit of the whole free public library movement as would be the making of the public schools an institution for the creation of Greek philologians. Everyone engaged in educational work, and especially those thus engaged who are most thoroughly equipped for the work in a literary way, and are most in touch with the literary and scholarly spirit, should have his attention called again and again to the needs of the crowd, the mass, the common people, the general run, the 90 per cent who either have never been within a schoolroom, or left it forever by the time they were thirteen years of age. And his attention should be again and again called to the fact that of the millions of children who are getting an education in this country today, not over 5 or 6 per cent at the outside, and perhaps even less than that, ever get as far, even, as the high schools. The few, of course, rule and must keep the lamp burning, but the many must have sufficient education to know how to walk by it if democracy is to endure. And the school for the many is, and is to be, if the opinions of librarians are correct, the free public library; but it cannot be a school for the many unless the many walk into it, and go among its books, handle them, and so doing come to know them and to love them and to use them, and to get wisdom from them.

CHAPTER XXXV

Advice to a librarian

[From Public Libraries, June, 1897]

As a matter of fact the position of librarian is more of an executive business affair than a literary one. Let me give you fair warning—it is in no sense your business to dictate to others as to what they may or may not, should or should not, read, and if you attempt to assume such responsibility you will make unnumbered enemies, and take upon yourself a thankless and uncalled-for task.

Frankly, do you know what is good for me to read? Are you not very much in doubt what is best for yourself? Isn't there a doubt in the best and most candid minds upon this same subject? Let the board of directors assume the responsibilities, work carefully and cautiously for the things that are considered best by persons of some authority, the people with sound, healthy bodies and clean minds, and thoroughly distrust the literary crank. Don't be too sure of your own judgment; the other fellow may be right, especially as to what he wants and needs.

Hang on to your tastes and prejudices for yourself, but don't impose them upon others. Cultivate your own tastes carefully by reading but little, and that little of the best; avoid the latest sensation until you are quite sure it is more than a sensation; if you have to buy it to please the patrons, have some convenient (literary) dog of good appetite and digestive organs, and try it on him or her and watch the general effect. You will be astonished how much you will find out about a book, its morals and manners, by the things they don't say. Our mutual friend's father, Mr D——, used to utterly damn a book to me when he said it was Just fair, and his It's a likely story, put things in the front ranks. Just get the confidence of as many readers as you can, grapple some of the most divergent minds with hooks of steel, and in finding out how little you know that is of any real value to anyone else, you will begin to be of some little value to yourself. Don't try to direct. The fellow that wants your direction will cause you to ooze out the information he needs, and you will hardly know that you have told him anything.

I may be, and doubtless am, saying much that is quite unnecessary, but I have tried to bear in mind some of my own mistakes, and of others around me. I have been impressed with the fact that librarians seem to think that they must or ought to know everything, and get to think they do know. It is a delusion. One can't know it all, and only a hopeless case tries.

Be more than content to be ignorant on many things. Look at your position as a high-grade business one, look after the working details, have things go smoothly, know the whereabouts and classification of the books, and let people choose their own mental food, but see to it that all that is put before them is wholesome.

CHAPTER XXXVI

The librarian as a host

Maude R. Henderson, in Public Libraries, September, 1896

Each librarian needs to have an ideal for society; must have before him an end of which his work will be only a part.

It is the peculiar position of the librarian to be so situated that with the consent of his trustees he may, simply by virtue of his office, be able to draw about him more of the elements of usefulness than almost any other person. Even a librarian who is a stranger is not taking matters unduly into his own hands in immediately availing himself of this privilege, for he is placed in the community where he can bring together those who have something to give and those who wish to receive. His invitation is non-partisan, non-sectarian, and without social distinctions.

The object of this article upon the librarian as a host is to suggest methods of usefulness for the community through the forms of entertainment at the disposal of the librarian. A surprising number of people, not having attractive surroundings, and not having unbounded resources within themselves, lead dull lives. The theater is expensive, sometimes not available, often not attractive, and one of the attractions of a library evening will be that it is "some place to go," but does no violence either to their scruples or their ideas of economy. Many who will not identify themselves with clubs, from an aversion to organization, will appreciate the freedom from it here, for there will be no officers, no rules, no fees.

If there is no especial note that the librarian thinks it would be well to sound, he may let it be known that the first of a series of entertainments to be given by the library, at the library, will be, for instance, a talk upon the Child in History, Our American Illustrators, or some attractive subject.

There are always a number of specialists, even in small places, who can contribute liberally to these plans, thus relieving the librarian of any real work beyond that of planning, while it accomplishes the double purpose of engaging the interest of the speaker in the work of the library, and of furnishing the entertainment for others. The following suggestions, which have been prepared for the work of a small library, will give a more definite idea of the plan.

Very often there will be found some one who, having a special fondness for one school of art, has made a collection of reproductions of its famous works in photographs, casts or engravings, who will willingly loan them for the illustration of a talk upon this theme, even if not quite as willingly giving the talk himself.

A beautiful program for a musical evening would consist of the conversation or paper upon a certain musical form, such as the opera, symphony, or perhaps dance music, being illustrated and varied by the performance of examples of those forms. The organized musical clubs could here be of the greatest service in taking charge of the whole entertainment.

An enthusiasm for a work of this kind may be somewhat crushed out by the press of regular duties, but the librarian may be greatly helped by the coöperation of organized clubs. Musical societies, Saengerbunds, the Elks, Daughters of the Revolution, and other societies are constantly preparing excellent entertainments, which it is hoped they will be willing to reproduce for those who have either not the leisure or the inclination to study. Such a movement does not in any way divert the energies of the library from their original aims, but is only another means of enhancing their efficacy. The resources of the library upon each of the subjects presented can be made known in many ways familiar to the librarian, such as posted lists, bulletins, and by the mention of them in the talks.

Upon a night which the librarian might consider of interest to them, special invitations may be sent to the different organized societies of working people, such as the retail clerks, labor unions, etc , who might not include themselves readily in a general published invitation.

It has been generally observed that more people re willing to read than know *what* to read, and are always glad of help in selection.

The originality of the librarian will develop many themes and schemes, and the work itself will doubtless show new veins which may be followed up. It may be that not many will avail themselves of any one invitation, but with a constant change of topic and manner of presentation, there cannot fail to be a great number, eventually, whose attention will be enlisted.

CHAPTER XXXVII

Library patrons—Making friends of them

Library patrons may be roughly divided into classes, thus: First—The adult student who, on rare occasions, calls to supplement the resources of his own collection of books with the resources of the public institution. This class is very small. Second—The dilettante, or amateur, who is getting up an essay or a criticism for some club or society, and wishes to verify his impression as to the color of James Russell Lowell's hair, or the exact words Dickens once used to James T. Fields in speaking of a certain ought-to-be-forgotten poem of Browning's. This class is large, and its annual growth in this country is probably an encouraging sign of the times. It indicates interest. Third—The serious-minded reader who alternately tackles Macaulay, Darwin, and Tom Jones with frequent and prolonged relapses—simply to rest his mind—into Mrs Wistar and Capt. King. This class is quite large, and though in too large a measure the victims of misplaced confidence in Sir John Lubbock and Frederick Harrison, they make excellent progress and do much to keep up the reading habit. Fourth—The "Oh, just-anything-good-you-know" reader. Her name is legion. She never knows what she has read. Yet the social student who failed to take into account the desultory, pastime reader, would miss a great factor in the spread of ideas. Fifth—The person who does not read. He is commoner than most suppose. He is often young, more often boy than girl, oftener young man than young woman. He commits eternally what Mr Putnam aptly calls the great crime against the library of staying away from it. He is classed among the patrons of the library somewhat as the western schoolma'am brought in knowledge of the capital of Massachusetts as part of her mental baggage: "Well, I know I ought to know it." He ought to be a library patron. How make him one? There are many methods, and all should be tried. The Pears' soap plan of printers' ink is one of the finest and best.

If a library has or is a good thing for the community let it so be said, early, late, and often, in large, plain type. So doing shall the library's books enter—before too old to be of service—into that state of utter worn-out-ness which is the only known book-heaven. Another way, and by some found good, is to work the sinfully indifferent first up into a library missionary, and then transform him into a patron. A library is something to which he can give an old book, an old paper, an old magazine, with no loss to himself. Having given, the library is at once his field, a Timbuctoo for his missionary spirit, is in part his creation. Ever after he is its interested friend. He wants to know about it. He goes to see it. He uses it.

CHAPTER XXXVIII
Public libraries and recreation
W. I. Fletcher in Public Libraries, July, 1898

There is nothing out of place in the comparing of the library to the school and the college, but its true mission is not to be so limited. To a large extent it is to be compared, as an object of public care and expense, with the park, the modern common, where there are flower-beds, rare plants in conservatories, lakes with boats in summer and skating in winter, and music by excellent bands. Not very strictly useful, these things, but recognized everywhere as ministering to the real culture of the people. Let this library, then, be the place where you will come, not merely to study and store your minds with so-called "useful" knowledge, but also often to have a good time; to refresh your minds and hearts with humor and poetry and fiction. Let the boys find here wholesome books of adventure, and tales such as a boy likes; let the girls find the stories which delight them and give their fancy and imagination exercise; let the tired housewife find the novels which will transport her to an ideal realm of love and happiness; let the hard-worked man, instead of being expected always to read "improving" books of history or politics, choose that which shall give him relaxation of mind and nerve, perhaps the Innocents abroad, or Josh Billings' "Allminax," or Samanthy at Saratoga.

CHAPTER XXXIX

Books as useful tools

There is still too much of superstition and reverence mingled with the thought of books and literature, and study and studentship in the popular mind. Books are tools, of which here and there one is useful for a certain purpose to a certain person. The farmer consults his farm paper on the mixing of pig-feed; the cook takes from the latest treatise the rules for a new salad; the chemist finds in his journal the last word on the detection of poisons; the man of affairs turns to the last market reports for guidance in his day's transactions; and all have used books, have studied literature. The hammer and the poem, the hoe and the dictionary, the engine and the encyclopedia, the trowel and the treatise on philosophy—these are tools. One and all, they are expressions of the life of the race. But they are not, for that reason, to be reverenced. They are proper for man's service, not man for theirs. Approach books, then, as you would a sewing machine, a school, or a factory.

Literature, after all, is simply all that's printed. In print are found the sum of the experience and observation of the whole race. Out of this print it is the librarian's business to help his fellows to draw such facts and suggestions as may aid them in their work.

CHAPTER XL

A village library successfully managed
James R. Garfield, in Public Libraries, October, 1896

Mentor, Ohio, is a village of but 500 people; therefore we are somewhat limited in our ability to raise funds for carrying on library work. But some six years ago 15 of us got together and began holding a series of meetings every month, something in the nature of the old New England township meeting, for the purpose of stirring up an interest in town affairs, and in doing that we considered it necessary to have some central point of interest around which we could all work, and we chose as that the library. There had never been a library in the village except a small circulating library. We all believed that the use of books and the greater knowledge of books would be a common center of interest around which we could all work and toward which we would be glad to give work. The result of five years' work in this way was that we now have a library of about 1600v., and two years ago, acting under a general law of the state, we became incorporated, and requested the village council to levy a tax for the work of the library. We at that time had about 1000v. The council very readily saw the advantage of this kind of work. They appreciated what was being done for the citizens and schools of the state, and therefore they levied a tax and turned the proceeds of the tax over to the library board. In this way, you will see, the library board is kept entirely aloof from politics. There are no elections by the people, nor is the board appointed by any political officers. It is a self-constituted body, a corporate body under the laws of this state, and as long as we maintain our corporate existence the village may turn over the funds to the library. We settled the difficulty of women's rights by having an equal number of both men and women on the board, and then in order to avoid the question of disruption of families we made the other member of the family who was not on an honorary member of the board. In this way we increased the number of workers and at the same time satisfied the desire of many people to hold office.

But we found that 15, together with the supernumerary and honorary members, were unwieldy, and the work practically devolved upon very few of the members. Therefore, when we incorporated, we made an executive board consisting of five members, and they had absolute management of the library proper. They are elected every year from the members of the association, and have absolute control of the library.

Although our library is supported by the village, we make it absolutely free to anyone who desires to use it. Those outside the village or township are required to put up a nominal deposit, merely for the safe return of the book. We made this the ideal toward which we are working—that the friendship of books is like the friendship of men, it is worth nothing and avails nothing unless it is used constantly and improved constantly.

CHAPTER XLI

Rules for the public

Printed rules, telling the public how they may use the library, are best put in the form of information and suggestions. Thus published they do not give the impression of red tape and restrictions so much as of help in making access to the library's resources easier and pleasanter.

The following suggestions and rules are copied with slight modification from a set in actual use.

The Utopia free public library
Information and suggestions

GENERAL

The library is open to everyone.

Do not hesitate to ask questions.

Suggestions of books for purchase and of changes in methods are asked for.

CIRCULATING DEPARTMENT

The circulating department is open from 10 to 9.

All persons residing in the city of Utopia, and giving satisfactory reference, are entitled to use the circulating department of the library on subscribing to the following agreement:

I hereby certify that I am a resident of the city of Utopia, and, in consideration of the right to use the free circulating department of the library, agree to comply with the regulations provided for its government.

A card-holder is responsible for all books taken on his card.

Immediate notice should be given of change of residence.

The library card should be presented when a book is drawn, renewed, or returned.

To renew a book, bring or send your card and the number of the book.

Lost cards can be replaced at once on payment of 10 cents for renewal, or without charge after a delay of two weeks.

One book, or one work if not in more than three volumes, may be taken at a time and kept two weeks, when it may be renewed for two weeks.

Four weeks is the limit of time that a book can be retained in any one household.

Books must be returned on the same card on which they are drawn.

A book cannot be transferred from one account to another unless it is brought to the library.

A fine at the rate of 2 cents per day is assessed on each book retained over time, payable on its return.

A book retained more than a week beyond the time limited may be sent for at the expense of the delinquent.

Books marked with a * in the catalogs are reference books, and are not lent.

No pen or pencil marks should be made in the books.

Any person who refuses to pay the fines or expenses mentioned, or wilfully violates any of the foregoing rules, forfeits thereby all right to the use of the library.

Teachers, and for good cause others, can take out more than one book (other than fiction) at a time, for such a term as may have been agreed upon before the books leave the library. In the absence of such agreement the books can be kept for the usual time only.

Persons not resident in the city may be allowed, at the discretion of the librarian, to take books on payment of $1 per year, and on signing an agreement to comply with the regulations of the library.

REFERENCE DEPARTMENT

The librarian and assistants are glad of opportunities to help those wishing to do reference work of any kind to a knowledge of the location of the books and the use of catalogs, indexes, and other aids.

READING ROOM

The reading room is open from 9 a.m. to 9 p.m. on week days; and on Sundays from 1 p.m. to 6 p.m.

Conversation and conduct inconsistent with quiet and order are prohibited.

Back numbers of papers and periodicals may be had on application to the attendants.

The books, papers, and periodicals should be carefully used, and neither marked nor cut.

Persons who wilfully violate any of the foregoing rules thereby forfeit all right to the use of the reading room.

CHAPTER XLII

Rules for the government of the Board of trustees and employes of the public library

[Slightly modified from the rules of the Erie (Pa.) public library.]

ARTICLE I
MEETINGS OF THE BOARD

Section 1. The regular meetings of the board of trustees shall be held on the Monday preceding the first Thursday of every month, at 8 p. m.

Sec. 2. Special meetings shall be called by the president whenever, in his judgment, they may be necessary; or at the written request of three members of the board.

ARTICLE II
QUORUMS

Section 1. Five members of the board and two of any standing committee shall constitute a quorum, in either case, for the transaction of business.

ARTICLE III
ORDER OF BUSINESS

Section 1. The order of business at all regular meetings of the board shall be as follows:
  1. Roll call.
  2. Reading of the minutes.
  3. Petitions and communications.
  4. Hearing of citizens and others.
  5. Report of the secretary.
  6. Report of the librarian.

7. Report of the book committee.
8. Report of the finance committee.
9. Report of the building committee.
10. Report of special committees.
11. Bills and pay-rolls.
12. New business.

ARTICLE IV
OFFICERS

Section 1. The officers of the board shall consist of a president, vice-president, and secretary, each of whom shall be elected at the regular meeting in January, to serve for one year. In case of a vacancy the board may elect a person to fill the unexpired term at any regular meeting. Temporary appointments may be made in the absence of the regular officers.

Sec. 2. The president shall preside at the meetings of the board; appoint the various committees; certify all bills that have been recommended for payment by the board; prepare the annual report; see to the general enforcement of the rules; and perform such other duties as the board may direct. In conjunction with the finance committee, he shall make an estimate at the close of each fiscal year of the probable expenses for the ensuing year, and submit the same to the board for its action.

Sec. 3. The vice-president shall perform the duties of the president in the latter's absence.

Sec. 4. The secretary shall record all proceedings of the board; read the minutes of the preceding meeting, or meetings, at each regular meeting; keep a detailed account of receipts and expenses; report the same to the board monthly; file all communications, vouchers, and other papers; certify all bills that have been recommended for payment by the board; transmit all resolutions and recommendations that may require it to the board of education or the proper committee thereof; prepare an annual report of receipts and expenses; and perform such other duties as the board may require.

ARTICLE V
COMMITTEES

Section 1. The standing committees of the board shall be a finance committee, a book committee, and a committee on building and grounds, each to consist of three members, to be named by the president at the regular meeting in February of each year.

Sec. 2. The finance committee shall certify to the correctness of all bills and pay-rolls before their presentation to the board; require a voucher for all expenses; see that the accounts are properly kept; aid the president in making up his annual estimates; verify the fiscal reports of the secretary and librarian; and look after the financial affairs of the board generally.

Sec. 3. The book committee shall be consulted by the librarian in the selection of all books, magazines, newspapers, etc.; prepare the rules for the management of the library; supervise the cataloging, labeling, and shelving of the various publications; have general charge of the book rooms; suggest suitable persons for employés (except the janitor and his assistants), and fix the duties of the same; require a list of all gifts, purchases and losses to be kept by the librarian, and verify his monthly and annual statements of the same.

Sec. 4. The committee on building and grounds shall purchase and take charge of the furniture and fixtures in the Library building; look after all matters pertaining to the building and grounds (inclusive of sidewalks, lawns, heating, lighting, and ventilation), and suggest the proper persons to serve as janitor and assistants to the same. They shall require all parts of the premises to be kept in a neat, clean, and creditable condition, and report all defects that require repair or remedy.

ARTICLE VI

EXPENDITURES

Section 1. Unless otherwise ordered by the board, no indebtedness shall be incurred without the previous approval of the proper committee.

Sec. 2. No committee shall authorize an expense of more than $25 in any one month without having secured the sanction of the board in advance.

Sec. 3. No bill shall be recommended to be paid by the board until it has been approved by the proper committee in writing.

Sec. 4. All bills recommended for payment by the board shall be certified by the president and secretary.

Sec. 5. When bids are asked for supplies, furniture, repairs, labor, etc., they shall be made under seal, and shall only be opened at a meeting of the board or of the committee to which the matter has been referred.

ARTICLE VII

TO BE IN WRITING

Section 1. All reports, recommendations, and resolutions shall be submitted in writing.

Sec. 2. Reports of committees shall be signed by two members thereof.

ARTICLE VIII
EMPLOYÉS

Section 1. The terms of all regular employés shall continue until their successors are appointed. They shall be subject, however, to removal for cause, at any time, by a vote of the board.

Sec. 2. The president may suspend any employé, for cause, subject to the action of the board at its next meeting.

Sec. 3. The salaries of employés shall be fixed before their election.

ARTICLE IX
THE LIBRARIAN

Section 1. Subject to the direction of the board and the several committees, the librarian shall have supervisory charge, control, and management of the Library building and all of its appurtenances, as well as of all the employés in and about the same.

Sec. 2. He shall be held strictly responsible for the care and preservation of the property in charge of the board; the courtesy and efficiency of the library service; the accuracy of the records; the reliability of his accounts and statements; the classifying, cataloging, and shelving of the books; the enforcement of the rules; the cleanliness and good condition of the building, grounds, and sidewalks; and the proper heating, lighting, and ventilation of the building.

Sec. 3. He shall attend the meetings of the board and assist the secretary in keeping his minutes and accounts.

Sec. 4. He shall keep an account, in permanent

form, of all his receipts and expenses on behalf of the library, and report the same to the board monthly.

Sec. 5. He shall make a monthly report of the operations of the library, including a list of all accessions to the various departments of the same, whether by gift or purchase, with such recommendations as, in his opinion, will promote its efficiency.

Sec. 6. He shall keep record books of all accessions to the library by purchase, and of all gifts for its several departments, with the dates when received, and, in the case of donations, the names and places of residence of the donors.

Sec. 7. He shall promptly and courteously acknowledge all gifts to the library or any of its departments.

Sec. 8. He shall keep an account of the time of the several employés; prepare the pay-rolls in accordance therewith, and place the same before the finance committee in advance of each regular meeting.

Sec. 9. He shall prepare an annual report showing, as fully as may be practical, the operation of the library and its several departments during the preceding year, with an inventory of the furniture, books, and other contents of the building.

Sec. 10. The first assistant librarian shall perform the duties of the librarian during the latter's absence.

ARTICLE X

AMENDMENTS

Section 1. Amendments hereto shall only be made at a regular meeting of the board, and must be proposed at least one month previous to final action on the same.

CHAPTER XLIII

Reports

As far as the welfare of the library is concerned, the money spent in publishing an elaborate annual report can often be better invested in a few popular books, or, better still, in a few attractively printed statements of progress and of needs, distributed through the community on special occasions. If there must be an annual report for the general public—which will not read it—it should be brief and interesting, without many figures and without many complaints. Do not think it necessary, in making up your report, to adopt the form or the list of contents usually followed by libraries. Give the necessary figures as briefly as may be, and adapt the rest of the report to the library and its community.

CHAPTER XLIV
Library legislation
Frank C. Patten, librarian Helena (Mont.) public library

The modern library movement is embodying ideas that are yet to make public libraries about as common as public schools, and correspondingly important in educational value. After a generation of most remarkable growth of public libraries in number, size, and recognized usefulness, experience can now enlighten us in regard to plans of library support and organization. The best interests of the movement are served by embodying the results of this experience in law. Such a law, by setting forth a good plan, encourages the establishment and promotes the growth of these popular educational institutions.

Outline of a good law

The following outline (with explanatory notes) embraces the important provisions of a good state library law:

1 *Establishment and maintenance.*—Authorize the governing body in connection with the voters of any city, town, county, school district, or other political body that has power to levy and collect taxes, to establish and maintain a public library for the free use of the people. Provide also for joint establishment and maintenance, for aiding a free library with public money, and for contract with some existing library for general or special library privileges. Provide for maintenance by regular annual rate of tax. Authorize special tax

or bonds to provide rooms, land, or buildings. Provide that on petition of 25 or 50 taxpayers the questions of establishment, rate of tax, and bonds shall first be decided by vote of the people at general or special election, to be changed only by another vote.

Note.—It is believed that there need be no limit of rate placed in the state law, as a community is not at all likely to vote to tax itself too high for library support. The people of a small place will, in fact, often fail to realize that in order to raise money enough to accomplish their object the tax rate must be higher than in a large place. It is not impossible that communities will, by and by, spend about as much in support of their public libraries as in support of their public schools.

2 *Management.*—Establish an independent board of trustees and place the management wholly in its hands. Constitute the library a public corporation, with power to acquire, hold, transfer, and lease property, and to receive donations and bequests. Secure a permanent board with gradual change of membership, the number of members to be not less than three, and the term of office certainly to be not less than three years.

Note.—In order to remove public library management from the influences of party politics, the library and its property should be wholly left to the control of trustees selected from citizens of recognized fitness for such a duty. Ex-officio membership in a library board should generally be avoided, especially in case of a small board; fitness for the position alone should be considered. Experience seems to show that in cities the proper board of trustees can best be secured through appointment by the mayor and confirmation by the council. It is a good way to provide for five trustees, one to be appointed each year for a term of five years. This number is large enough to be representative, and small enough to avoid the great difficulty in securing a quorum if the number is large. The length of term in connection with gradual change of membership encourages careful planning, and it secures the much needed continuity of management and political independence. And yet there is sufficient change of officers so that the board will not be too far removed from the public will.

3 *Miscellaneous.*—State the purpose of a public library broadly, perhaps in the form of a definition. Make possible the maintenance of loan, reference, reading room, museum, lecture, and allied educational features, and of branches. Prescribe mode for changing form of organization of an existing library to conform to new law. Impose penalties for theft, mutilation, over-detention, and disturbance. Provide for distributing all publications of the state free to public libraries.

Note.—It is probably most convenient to have the library year correspond with the calendar year. It is well to have the trustees appointed and the report of the library made at a different time of the year from either the local or general elections. The library is thus more likely to be free from the influences of party politics. To have a library treasurer is probably the better plan, but library money may be kept in the hands of the municipal treasurer as a separate fund, and be paid out by order of the board of trustees only.

Libraries for schoolrooms, to be composed of reference books, books for supplementary reading, class duplicates, and professional books for teachers, should be provided for in the public school law. School funds should be used and school authorities should manage these libraries. The business of lending books for home use is better and more economically managed by a public library, having an organization that is independent of the school authorities.

4 *A state central authority.*—Establish a state library commission; appointments on this commission to be made by the governor and confirmed by the senate, one each year for a term of five years. Make the commission the head of the public library system of the state with supervisory powers. Let the commission

manage the state library entirely, and center all its work at that institution. Let it be the duty of the commission, whenever it is asked, to give advice and instruction in organization and administration to the libraries in the state; to receive reports from these libraries and to publish an annual report; to manage the distribution of state aid, and to manage a system of traveling libraries.

Note.—Within a few years each of several states has provided for a state library commission, to be in some sense the head of the public library system of the state, as the state board of education is the head of the public school system of the state. By having small traveling libraries of 50 or 100v. each, to lend for a few months to localities that have no libraries, and by having a little state aid to distribute wisely, the state library commission is able to encourage communities to do more for themselves in a library way than they otherwise would. There may be cases where the work of the commission might better be centered at the state university library. The state library commission has proved to be a useful agency wherever tried, and the plan seems likely to spread throughout the country. In Wyoming the income from 30,000 acres of state land forms a library fund. It would seem probable that other states will adopt this plan. By far the most complete and successful state system that has yet been organized is that of New York, where all centers in the state library at Albany as headquarters.

Reading matter on library legislation

The report of the United States commissioner of education for 1895–96 contains a compilation of the library laws of all the states. Every year new laws and amendments are enacted in several of the states, and the advance is very marked. The laws of New York, Massachusetts, Wisconsin, and Illinois are among the best.

Essentials of a good law

The three most essential things to be provided for in a good state library law are:

1 A sure and steady revenue.
2 Careful and consecutive management.
3 A central library authority.

In attempting to alter or make new laws, these essentials should be kept clearly in mind, but special conditions peculiar to each state dictate modifications of any general plan. Anyone interested in the matter could read the general articles upon the subject and the various state laws, and then, with the assistance of the best legal talent to be obtained, frame an act appropriate to the conditions of his state.

CHAPTER XLV
A. L. A. and other library associations and clubs

The American Library Association was organized in 1876. It holds annual meetings. It publishes its proceedings in volumes, of which those now in print may be purchased of the A. L. A. Publishing section, 10½ Beacon st., Boston, or of the secretary. It seeks in every practicable way to develop and strengthen the public library as an essential part of the American educational system. It therefore strives by individual effort of members, and where practicable by local organization, to stimulate public interest in establishing or improving libraries, and thus to bring the best reading within reach of all.

Librarians, trustees, and persons interested may become members; the annual fee is $2. Membership entitles one to a copy of the proceedings; it has now about 800 members.

Every person actively engaged in library work owes it to herself, as well as to her profession, to join the American Library Association. If the association is large, if its meetings are well attended, if its proceedings as published show that the problems of library work are carefully studied, if the published proceedings are widely circulated, it is easier to persuade the intelligent part of the public that the librarian's profession is serious, dignified, and calls to its membership men and women of ability and zeal. If the public is persuaded of these things, the position of the humblest as well as of the highest in the profession is thereby rendered better worth the holding. To attend diligently to one's business is sometimes a most proper form of advertising one's merits. To be a zealous and active member of the A. L. A. is to attend to an important part of one's business; for one can't join it and work with it and for it and not increase one's efficiency in many ways.

State associations have been organized in the following states: New York, Pennsylvania, Ohio, Wisconsin, Maine, Massachusetts, Michigan, Minnesota, Nebraska, New Hampshire, New Jersey, Vermont, California, Colorado, Connecticut, Georgia, Illinois, Indiana, Iowa.

The following states have state library commissions: Connecticut, Georgia, Massachusetts, New Hampshire, New York, Ohio, Vermont, Wisconsin, Indiana, Colorado, Michigan, New Jersey, Minnesota.

The following cities have library clubs: Buffalo, Chicago, Minneapolis, New York city, Washington city.

An inquiry for information regarding any of these associations or clubs, addressed to any librarian in the states given, will receive attention.

Much of what is said above about the A. L. A. applies with equal force to the association of one's state or neighborhood. Often, moreover, it is possible to attend a state association meeting at small expense of time or money.

CHAPTER XLVI

Library schools and training classes

As libraries have become more thoroughly organized, as they have become more aggressive in their methods, and as they have come to be looked upon by librarians and others as possible active factors in educational work, the proper management of them has naturally been found to require experience and technical knowledge as well as tact, a love of books, and janitorial zeal. It is seen that the best librarians are trained as well as born; hence the library school. The library school—a list of those now in operation will be found at the end of this chapter—does not confine itself to education in the technical details of library management. It aims first to arouse in its pupils the "modern library spirit," the wish, that is, to make the library an institution which shall help its owners, the public, to become happier and wiser, and adds to this work what it can of knowledge of books, their use, their housing, and their helpful arrangement. Perhaps the ideal preparation for a librarian today would be, after a thorough general education, two or three years in a good library school preceded and followed by a year in a growing library of moderate size.

A few libraries have tried with much success the apprentice system of library training, taking in a class, or series of classes, for a few months or a year, and at the end of the period of apprenticeship selecting from the class additions to its regular corps.

List of library schools and training classes

New York state library school, Albany; Pratt institute library school, Brooklyn; Wisconsin summer school of library science, Madison; Drexel institute library school, Philadelphia, Pa.; University of Illinois state library school, Champaign; Amherst summer school library class, Amherst, Mass.; Los Angeles public library training class; Cleveland summer school of library science.

CHAPTER XLVII

The Library department of the N. E. A.

The Library department of the National educational association holds meetings annually at the same time and place with the N. E. A.

The National educational association is the largest organized body of members of the teaching profession in the world. Its annual meetings bring together from 5000 to 15,000 teachers of every grade, from the kindergarten to the university. It includes a number of departments, each devoted to a special branch of educational work. The Library department was established in 1897. It has held successful meetings. It is doing much to bring together librarians and teachers. It is arousing much interest in the subject of the use of books by young people, briefly touched on in the later chapters of this book.

Following the example of the N. E. A., many state and county associations of teachers throughout the country have established library departments. At these are discussed the many aspects of such difficult and as yet unanswered questions as: What do children most like to read? How interest them in reading? What is the best reading for them?

CHAPTER XLVIII

Young people and the schools

If possible give the young people a reading room of their own, and a room in which are their own particular books. These special privileges will not bar them from the general use of the library. Make no age limit in issuing borrowers' cards. A child old enough to know the use of books is old enough to borrow them, and to begin that branch of its education which a library only can give. The fact that a child is a regular attendant at school is in itself almost sufficient guarantee for giving him a borrower's card. Certainly this fact, in addition to the signature of parent, guardian, or adult friend, even if the signer does not come to the library, will be guarantee enough.

Teachers should be asked to help in persuading children to make the acquaintance of the library, and then to make good use of it. To get this help from teachers is not easy. They are generally fully occupied with keeping their pupils up to the required scholarship mark. They have no time to look after outside matters.

Visits to teachers in their schoolrooms by librarian or assistant will often be found helpful. Lists of books adapted to schoolroom use, both for the teacher and for pupils, are good, but are very little used when offered, unless followed up by personal work. Brief statements of what the library can do and would like to do in the way of helping on the educational work of the community will be read by the occasional teacher. Teachers can sometimes be interested in a library through the interest in it of the children themselves. The work of getting young people to come to the library and enjoy its books should go hand in hand with the work of persuading teachers to interest children in the library. It is not enough to advertise the library's advantages in the papers, or to send to teachers a printed statement that they are invited and urged to use the institution; nor is it enough to visit them and say that the books in the library are at their service. These facts must be demonstrated by actual practice on every possible opportunity. A teacher who goes to a library and finds its privileges much hedged about with rules and regulations will perhaps use it occasionally, certainly not often. Appropriate books should be put directly into their hands, the educational work of this, that, and the other teacher should be noted, and their attention called to the new books which touch their particular fields.

Teachers' cards can be provided which will give to holders special privileges. It is a question, however, if such a system is necessary or worth while. Under the charging system already described any teacher can be permitted to take away as many books as she wishes, and a record of them can be easily and quickly made. To give "teachers' cards," with accompanying privileges, is to limit to some extent the rights of all others. And yet teachers may very often properly receive special attention. In a measure they are part of the library's staff of educational workers. But these special attentions or favors should be offered without proclaiming the fact to the rest of the community.

Many cannot see why a teacher should receive favors not granted to all.

Take special pains to show children the use of indexes, and indeed of all sorts of reference books; they will soon be familiar with them and handle them like lifelong students. Gain the interest of teachers in this sort of work, and urge them to bring their classes and make a study of your reference books.

CHAPTER XLIX

How the library can assist the school

Channing Folsom, superintendent of schools, Dover, N. H., in Public Libraries, May, 1898

We have to consider the teacher, the school, the pupil, the home. The teacher is likely to be conservative; to have fallen into ruts; to be joined to his idols; to make the text-book a fetish; to teach a particular book rather than the subject, so that the initiative in works of coöperation must come from the library side.

If, then, the library is equally conservative, if the librarian and the trustees look upon their books as too sacred or too precious to be handled by boys and girls, the desired coöperation will never be attained.

In beginning the desired work the librarian must have a well-defined idea of what is to be done and how. There should be a well-defined line of differentiation between material which the school should furnish and that properly belonging to the library province.

Of course all text-books, all supplementary reading matter for classroom use, all ordinary reference books, should be furnished by the school authorities. But the more extensive and the more expensive dictionaries, gazetteers, cyclopedias, and books for topical reference cannot be so furnished. If they are to be used by public school pupils, the library must supply them, and make access to them as easy and as pleasant as possible.

It is within the scope of the library to improve the taste in reading among the pupils of the schools by compiling lists of the best books upon the shelves, and distributing these lists to the pupils. Such lists may be classified as suitable to different grades or ages, or by subjects, as, History of different countries or epochs, Biography, Travels, Nature work, Fiction, etc.

The possible good that may be achieved in this way is immeasurable. Although, according to Dogberry, to write and read comes by nature, we must remember that a taste for good reading is not innate but acquired, and that it is not ordinarily acquired under unfavorable conditions. To ensure the acquirement of this taste by the child, good reading must be made as accessible as the bad, the librarian and the teacher must conspire to put good reading, interesting reading, elevating reading in his way. The well-read person is an educated person. The taste for good reading once acquired is permanent. There is little danger of backsliding. It grows with indulgence. One writer says: No man having once tasted good food or good wine, or even good tobacco, ever voluntarily turns to an inferior article. So with our reading habits; a taste for good reading once acquired becomes a joy forever.

Teachers do not realize, as does the librarian, the low tone of the reading taste of the community. When they fully understand this, together with the fact that the acquirement of a reading habit and a love for good literature are largely dependent, in a majority of cases, upon the public school training, then will the librarian have to bestir himself to supply the demand for good books made by the school.

The habit thus formed, the taste thus acquired, will be of infinitely more value to them than the information gained. The latter may soon be forgotten, the former will stay with them through life; but the influence of good books taken into the homes of our school children, from the library or from the school, does not stop with the children themselves. It is impossible that such books should go into even an ignorant, uncouth, unlettered family without exerting an elevating and refining influence.

Thus the school opens to the library the broadest field for doing the greatest good to the greatest number, the shortest avenue to the masses.

But the consciousness of good done will not be the only reward for the library. The reflex action upon the library of this intimate connection with the school will be highly beneficial. A generation will grow up trained to associate the library and the school as instrumentalities of public education, demanding alike its moral and financial support, a generation that in town meetings and in city councils will advocate generous appropriations for the public library as well as for the public school.

Thus, your bread cast upon the waters shall return unto you after many days.

CHAPTER L

Children's room

In recent years a number of the larger libraries of the country have given up a portion of the delivery room, or a separate room entire, to the use of children. All of these special arrangements for children thus far reported have been successful. The plan that seems to give the greatest satisfaction, is to place in a room opening from the delivery room, and perhaps forming in effect a part of it, the books in the library especially adapted to the use of young people up to about 14 years of age. Such of these books as are not fiction are classified as closely as are the books in the main part of the library, and are arranged by their numbers on the shelves.

In this room the children have free access to the shelves. An attendant in charge gives special attention to the wants of the young visitors, and as far as possible gives guidance in the selection and instruction in the use of the books. A collection of reference books adapted to the young is sometimes added to the books which circulate.

Even in the very small library a corner for young people will usually be found an attractive and useful feature. It draws the young folks away from the main collection, where their presence sometimes proves an annoyance. It does not at all prevent the use, by the younger readers, of the books of the elders if they wish to use them, and it makes much easier some slight supervision, at least, of the former's reading.

CHAPTER LI

Schoolroom libraries

"Schoolroom library" is the term commonly applied to a small collection, usually about 50v., of books placed on an open shelf in a schoolroom. In a good many communities these libraries have been purchased and owned by the board of education, or the school authorities, whoever they may be. If they are the property of the school board they commonly remain in the schoolroom in which they are placed. As the children in that room are changed each year, and as the collections selected for the different grades are usually different, the child as he passes through the rooms comes into close contact with a new collection each year. There are some advantages in having the ownership and control of these libraries remain entirely in the hands of the school board and the superintendent. The library, however, is generally the place in the community in which is to be found the greatest amount of information about books in general, the purchasing of them, the proper handling of them in fitting them for the shelves, cataloging, binding, etc., and the selection of those best adapted to young people. It is quite appropriate therefore, that, as is in many cities the case, the public library should supply the schools with these schoolroom libraries from its own shelves, buying therefor special books and often many copies of the same book.

If schoolroom libraries do come from the public

library, they can with very little difficulty be changed several times during the school year. With a little care on the part of the librarian and teachers, the collection of any given room can be by experience and observation better and better adapted to the children in that room as time goes on.

There are many ways of using the schoolroom library. The books forming it should stand on open shelves accessible to the pupils whenever the teacher gives permission. They may be lent to the children to take home. Thus used they often lead both children and parents to read more and better books than before, and to use the larger collections of the public library. They may be used for collateral reading in the schoolroom itself. Some of them may be read aloud by the teacher. They may serve as a reference library in connection with topics in history, geography, science, and other subjects.

Wherever introduced these libraries have been very successful.

CHAPTER LII

Children's home libraries

In a few cities the following plan for increasing the amount of good reading among the children of the poorer and less educated has been tried with great success. It is especially adapted to communities which are quite distant from the public library or any of its branches. It is, as will be seen, work which is in the spirit of the college settlement plan. The "home libraries," if they do no more, serve as a bond of common interest between the children and their parents, and the persons who wish to add to their lives something of interest and good cheer. As a matter of fact they do more than this. They lead not a few to use the library proper, and they give to at least a few boys and girls an opportunity for self-education such as no other institution yet devised can offer.

A home library is a small collection of books, usually only 15 or 20, with one or two young folks' periodicals, put up in a box with locked cover. The box is so made that it will serve as a bookcase and can be hung on a wall or stood on the floor or a table. In the neighborhood in which it is to be placed a group of four or five children is found—or perhaps a father or a mother—who will agree to look after the books. To one of these, called the librarian, is given the key of the box, and the box itself is placed in the spot selected; perhaps a hallway or a living room. Under a few very simple regulations the librarian lends the books in the home library to the young people of the neighborhood. If the experiment is successful the first set of books is changed for another, and the work continues. Or perhaps the library is enlarged; and perhaps even grows into a permanent institution.

CHAPTER LIII

Literary clubs and libraries

Evva L. Moore, Withers' public library

[Public Libraries, June, 1897]

In your community are a number of literary clubs; if there are not, it lies within the power of the librarian to create them: an evening club composed of men and women; a ladies' club for the study of household economics; a young ladies' club for the study of music or some literary topic; a club for young men in which to study sociology; a novel club for the study of the world's great fiction. For constitutions suitable for such clubs, account of administration, organization, etc., consult the Extension bulletin no. 11 of the university of the state of New York, and Bulletin no. 1, June, 1896, of the Michigan State library, and List of books for women and girls and their clubs.

The study club is one of the best means of extending the influence of your library; of securing the attention and hold of the people. It awakens thought, arouses discussions, puts into circulation books which otherwise might stand idle on the shelves.

It is necessary to study carefully the courses of study of the different clubs, and to do this the programs must be on file in the library. If they are printed (and encourage this) so much the better; if in manuscript they can be used with small inconvenience.

If the program is prepared week by week only, make arrangements to have it sent immediately to the library; also watch your local paper for notices.

No doubt the officers of the various clubs come to you for suggestions when arranging the course of study for the year, and to inquire as to the resources of the library on the subject in hand, in order that every effort may be made to fill the gaps in the library collection. When a request of this kind comes, suggestions and assistance may be obtained from the two bulletins mentioned above, as, in addition to information along the lines of organization, they contain outlines of study.

Harper's bazaar devotes a page each week to club women and club work. University-extension bulletins and courses of study offer numerous suggestions.

The literary clubs of the smaller towns without libraries, within a radius of a few miles of your own small town, copying after their more pretentious sister along literary lines, should have your encouragement and assistance. Lend all the books that you can spare, on as easy terms as are compatible with your rules; in short, institute traveling libraries on a small scale.

CHAPTER LIV

Museums, lectures, etc.

A museum in connection with the library, either historical or scientific, or an art gallery, may be made a source of attraction, and of much educational value. The collecting of antiquities, or natural history specimens, or rare bindings, or ancient books or manuscripts, is generally taken up by societies organized for such purposes. The library should try to bring these collections into such relations with itself as to add to its own attractiveness, and to make more interesting and instructive the collections.

A library can often very happily advertise itself, and encourage the use of its books, by establishing a series of lectures. Entertainments, somewhat of the nature of receptions, or exhibits of the library's treasures in the library itself, will sometimes add to the institution's popularity, and will always afford a good excuse for sending to leading people in the community a note reminding them of the library's existence and perhaps of its needs.

CHAPTER LV

Rules for the care of photographs

Henry W. Kent, Slater museum, Norwich, Conn.

I. Accessioning

The *accession book* should be ruled in columns under the following headings:

A, Accession number; B, Author; C, Title; D, Gallery; E, Photographer and place of publication; F, Date of publication; G, Photographer's number; H, Process; I, Size of print; J, Size of mount; K, Cost; L, Cost of mounting; M, Remarks.

A Accession number. The consecutive Museum number to be either written or printed. This column should be used to give the date of accession.

B Author. For photographs of paintings give one important name.

For photographs of sculpture give sculptor's name, where known.

For photographs of architecture give name of city followed by country in parentheses. London (Eng.)

C Title. For photographs of painting and sculpture use short, catch title, bringing, where possible, the important name first.

For photographs of architecture, make first word a word descriptive of the kind of building: Temple of Mars; Cathedral of Notre Dame; Basilica of S. Paolo.

D Gallery. This column is used for sculpture and painting only. Enter official name of gallery under name of city, followed by country in parentheses, and separated by hyphen: London (Eng.)-National Gallery; Paris (France)-Louvre.

E Photographer and place of publication. Use the last name of publisher, followed by name of city abbreviated. Alinari, Fio.; Braun, Pa.; Hanfstaengl, Mün.

F Date. The high grade photographs have the date of their publication on the mount.

G Publisher's number. To be found on all prints.

H Process. State whether silver print, platinotype, carbon (give color b. for black, br. for brown, g. for gray), autotype, collotype, etc.

I Size of print. Give size in centimeters, giving width first.

J Size of mount. Use the following notation:

F for size measuring 22x28 inches, and upwards.
Q for size measuring 18x22 inches up to 22x28.
O for size measuring 14x18 inches up to 18x22.
D for all sizes under O.

K Cost. Give cost of imported prints in foreign money; give total of bill in American money.

L Cost of mounting.

M Remarks. This column will be found useful for date of remounting prints.

Enter all prints in the order of the publisher's bill.

Write the accession number on the back of mount (see under Labeling) and on author card.

II. Card cataloging

Photographs of paintings and sculpture should be entered under the following heads: A, Author, B, Title, C, Gallery, D, School of painter or sculptor.

Use Library Bureau card, no. 33r.

A Author card. This should show, a, author's name, dates of birth and death, and school; b, Title of work;

c, Kind of work; d, Gallery; e, Imprint; f, Accession number; g, Classification or storage number.

Aa Enter author on first blue line between red lines, under his best known name, even if a nickname, giving full name with nicknames and their translations after it,

	Giorgione, Il. (Giorgio Barbarelli) called.		
	⁵/1477-1511.	Italian-Venetian	
		○	
A			

Painting card; author, with full name to precede list of words.

in parentheses. Give dates of birth and death in parentheses, followed by name of the school to which the artist belonged. Make cross-references from all forms under which the author might be looked for.

(It will be found convenient to give all this data on one card, to precede the list of the artist's works, using on all following cards the first, or well-known name, only.)

Ab Write the title on second blue line, at the right of red lines. Make it as brief as possible, using the

		2	
a	Giorgione, Il.		
G43h		⁶Holy Family.	Easel-picture.
	Venice (Italy) - Palazzo Giovanelli.		
		Naya, Venice. 993.	Silver, 27x35 cm.
.		○	
A			

Painting card; author, showing title of work, kind of work, gallery, etc.

important name in it, first. Christ, Baptism of; Christ, Betrayal of; Virgin Mary, Coronation of; St John, Birth of; St Peter, Martyrdom of.

Ac Indicate after the title whether it is an easel-picture, fresco, statue, relief, or a part of a larger work.

Ad Give on fourth blue line, at left of red lines, the official name of gallery, preceded by city, with country in parentheses. London (Eng.)-National Gallery.

Ae Give the imprint on fifth blue line, beginning at the right of red lines: name of photographer, place of publication, date, number of print, process, size of print in cm., bottom by height.

B Title card. This card should show, a, Title, b, Author.

		Holy Family.	See
	Buonarotti		Florence (It)-Palazzo Uffizi
Q-G43h	Giorgione. ll.		Venice (It)-Palazzo Giovanelli
	Ghirlandajo. ll.		Florence (It)-Palazzo Uffizi.
		O	
B			

Painting card; title, with different authors and galleries.

Ba Give on first blue line, beginning at the left of red lines, a full title, but as in Ab make the important name or word the first word. Christ, Baptism of; Christ, Betrayal of; St John, Birth of; Portrait of Pope Julius.

Bb Give on second blue line, between red lines, the one well known or important author's name; the first one used in Aa.

The title card becomes in most cases a series card, since the title of an often-represented subject attracts to itself many names of artists. In such cases arrange the authors' names alphabetically, in columns, and against them write the names of the galleries where the works are to be found. Give class and author number in blue ink at the left.

C Gallery card. This card is a series card, and should show, a, name of gallery; b, names of the artists and their works in the gallery.

Ca Give official name of gallery preceded by the name of the city where it is located, with country in parentheses.

Cb Enter alphabetically, names of authors, with the title of their works, one author to a line. Give at the left, classification numbers in blue ink.

```
                Venice (Italy) - Palazzo Giovanelli


 Q - G43h       Giorgione, Il.           Holy Family
        G
```

Painting card; gallery, with authors and titles of works.

D School card. This should show under the names American, English, French, German, Italian-Florentine, Italian-Venetian, Italian-Umbrian, Italian-Parmesan,

Spanish, etc., all the artists of the school arranged alphabetically, with the number of their works written in, in pencil.

	School	
	Italian-Venetian	
Q-G43h	Giorgione, il.	Veronese
	○	
D		

Painting card: school, all authors of school arranged alphabetically with number of works written in pencil.

Photographs of Architecture should be cataloged according to the foregoing rules, except in the following cases:

Author card. For author, give the name of the city where the building or detail is found, followed by the country in parentheses.

For title make the first word descriptive of the kind of building, and after the name of the building give the point from which the view was taken, affixed to the words interior or exterior: Temple of Zeus, Exterior from the east. Cathedral of Notre Dame, Interior of nave looking east.

Instead of gallery, give style of building, using words Egyptian, Assyrian, Greek, Roman, Byzantine, Romanesque, Gothic, Renaissance, Modern, etc., followed by adjective indicating country.

Imprint the same.

Gallery card will not be needed.

```
| O    | Poitiers (France)               |
| P75  | Cathedral.   Interior of Nave look-
                      ing East.
| Gothic | French.
|        | Robett, Paris. 348    Silver, 28x39 cm.
| A
```

Architecture card; author, showing place, kind of building, and style.

For school card use S style card.

Style card. This should show all photographs arranged by cities, under styles, under general term Architecture.

Architecture, Gothic—Italian.
Architecture, Gothic—Spanish.
Architecture, Gothic—English, perpendicular.
Architecture, Gothic—English, pointed.

```
|   | Architecture - Gothic        French.
|   | Abbeuville      Ch. of S. Wulfrand
|   | Amiens          Cathedral.
|   | Auxerre
| S |
```

Architecture card; style, showing place, etc.

The cards for the three divisions, architecture, painting, and sculpture, should be kept in separate alphabets.

III. Classification

Arrange the photographs of sculpture and painting alphabetically by authors where known; where not known, by subjects under the various sizes.

Arrange the photographs of architecture alphabetically by cities, under the sizes.

Indicate the arrangement on cards by two numbers, in blue ink: the Classification number and the Author number.

Classification number. This is indicated by the letters F, Q, O, D.

Author number. Use the C: A. Cutter Letter alphabetic-order table for book authors, and add to the number so gained the first one or two letters (as the number of prints may require) of the title of the print; or the numerals 1, 2, and 3 may be used.

Write these two numbers in blue ink on the cards, as follows:

Author card. Class number on the first line of upper left-hand corner; author number below it.

On other cards. Write at the left of first red line the two numbers on one line separated by a hyphen.

IV. Labeling

Give author's name in full, with dates, in parentheses, and school, beginning directly under left-hand corner of print.

Give title, same as on title card, only reversing the form, beginning under the middle of print and running out to the right-hand corner.

Some collections have more or less descriptive matter on the mount, but this is to be discouraged.

Give the Gallery or Style at lower left-hand corner of mount 1 inch from either edge. Use waterproof or India ink in all cases.

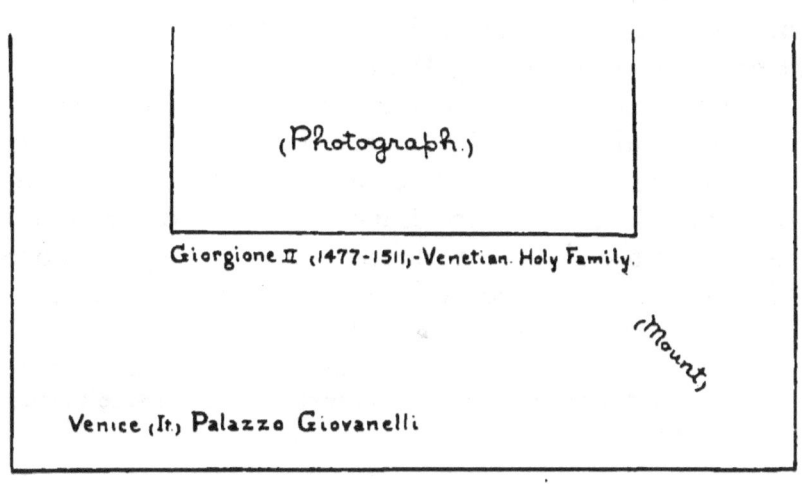

Showing proper method of entering descriptive matter on mounted photographs.

Stamp name of collection with rubber stamp on back of mount in upper left-hand corner, 1½ inches from upper and side edges.

The stamp should give full name and place of museum or library, leaving room above for class and author number, and below for accession number.

```
Class ——    Author ——
Slater Memorial Museum
      Norwich, Conn.
No. ——
```

V. Storage

Store sizes Q, O, and D, in drawers of a cabinet, which may be easily removed to table, or in pigeon-holes; stand the mounts on long edges, with backs to the front, so that classification and author numbers may be easily seen in turning them over.

Store size F in drawers, but lying flat. These should be taken out of the drawer and laid on a table when being handled. The drawers for the smaller sizes should be box-shaped, with sides cut down somewhat to allow the prints to be easily turned. Those for the large size should have no front, but the case containing them should have doors.

NOTE.—Be very careful in handling photographs never to rub or pull one over another; always turn them from side to side, like the leaves of a book.

INDEX

Accession book, 33, 77; for photographs, 171; sample page, 76.
Accession number for photographs, 171; in accession book, 76–77; on shelf list, 92; on catalog cards, 94.
Accessioning photographs, 171–172.
Additions, lists of, 93, 112.
Advertising a library, 10–11, 132, 158, 170.
Advice to a librarian, 125–126.
Age limit for borrowers, 157.
Agents, *see* Book dealers.
Agreement blanks, 33, 118–119.
Alphabetical arrangement, dictionary catalog, 96, 101; for photographs, 177–178.
Alphabets, 69; specimen page, 71.
Amendments to rules of library board, 146.
American catalog of books, 30.
A. L. A. catalog, 30.
American library association, fee, 152; members, 152-3; objects, 152.
Amherst summer school library class, 155.
Ancient manuscripts, collections, 170.
Annual literary index, 55.
Annual report, 146.
Antiquities, collections, 170.
Appointment of librarian, 20, 23, 25.
Appointment of library assistants, 18.
Appointment of trustees, 148.
Apprentice classes, 154.
Architecture card, author, 181; style, 181; title, 180.

Art entertainments, 129.
Art galleries, 170.
Assistant librarian, duties of, 145.
Associations, *see* Library associations.
Author card, 94; for architecture, 176–177; for painting and sculpture, 172–174.
Author catalog, 94–95.
Author-list, 95, 113.
Author-number, explained, 90; for photographs, 178; on shelf list, 92.
Author table, *see* Cutter author table.
Author's name, in accession book, 77; in catalog, 93; in shelf list, 92; on order slip, 64.
Baker, C. A., Reference books for a small library, 46–52.
Ballard's klips, 107.
Beginning work, things needed in, 30–34.
Beginnings of the library, 9–10.
Best books (Sonnenschein), 31.
Bills, checking, 64, 100.
Binders for magazines, 58–59.
Bindery-book, 102.
Bindery number, 102, 104.
Bindery schedule, 104–105.
Binding, 63, 102–105; materials, 102–103; cloth, 102–103; leather, 102, 104; sewing, 102–103; backs, 102–103; joints, 102–103; lettering, 104–105; titles and indexes, 105; advertisements, 105; periodicals, 104; folios, 103–104; newspapers, 103; fiction, 103; juveniles, 103; rules for, 105.

INDEX

Biography, classification of, 79.
Blanks, agreement, 33, 118-119; order slip, 63-64; request, 45, 65.
Board, *see* Trustees.
Book-buying, *see* Buying books.
Book committee, 142.
Book cards, 33, 114-115-116-117; *see also* Book slip.
Book dealers, 63, 66-67-68.
Book-lists, *see* Lists.
Book-mark, illustration, 116.
Book news (monthly), 32.
Book-numbers, 96.
Book-plates, 99-100.
Book-pockets, 33, 99-100, 114-115-116-117.
Book-reviews, 32, 100.
Book-slip, 99, 101; *see also* Book card.
Book supports, 73.
Books, as useful tools, 134; for girls and women and their clubs (Iles), 32; needed in beginning work, 30-32; overdue, 116; reference, *see* Reference books; renewal of, 116; selection of, *see* Selection of books.
Bookcases, 26-27; steel, 28; wooden, 28.
Borrowers, age limit, 157; cards for, 33, 114-115, 117-118, 157-158; index to, 119; information for, 137; numbers for, 115-116, 119; register of, 33, 116, 119-120; responsibility of, 118, 138.
Buildings and grounds committee, 142.
Buildings, library; *see* Library buildings.
Bulletins, 93, 101, 112, 130; *see also* Lists.
Buying books, 18, 63-68; ordering, 64, 67; agents, 63, 66-67-68; price, 65-66-67-68; discounts, 63, 65-66-67; editions, 63, 65-66-67; binding, type, quality of paper, 63; complete sets, 66; series, 66; second-hand books, 66, 68; fiction, 66; for children, 66-67; new books, 68; when to buy, 68; *see also* Selection of books.
Call-number, defined, 92; in book, 99, 101; on book-slip, 99, 101, 114; on pocket, 99, 101, 114; on label, 98-99, 101; in accession book, 92, 101; on shelf-list, 92; on catalog-cards, 94, 96; in charging system, 115.
Capitalization, 94.
Card catalog rules, 30, 94-96; for photographs, 172-177.
Card pocket, *see* Book pocket.
Care of books, brief rules for, 75; dusting books, 74; handling books, 74, 99-100; covering books, 75; cutting leaves, 74, 100; gas, heat, damp, 74.
Carter's ink, 34, 69.
Cases, *see* Bookcases; Catalog cases.
Catalog, arrangement of, 101; author, 94-95; dictionary, 96; duplicate, 94; on cards, 93; printed, 93, 113; of A. L. A. library, 30; subject headings for, 95-97; trays for holding, 97.
Catalog cards, 33, 93-97, 101.
Catalog case, 33, 97.
Catalog rules, 30, 93-97.
Cataloging books, 93-97.
Cataloging photographs, 172-177.
Chairs, 27-28.
Change of residence, 138.
Charging system explained, 115.
Check list of public documents, 109.
Checking bills, 64, 100.
Checking the library, 111.
Children's books, *see* Juvenile books.

INDEX

Children's cards, 157.
Children's home libraries, 166–167.
Children's privileges, 157.
Children's rooms, 157, 163.
Circulating department, 121, 137.
Class number, decimal, 81; expansive, 84; explained, 79; for photographs, 178; in accession book, 77; on shelf list, 92; in catalog, 93.
Classification, defined, 78; decimal, 79, 81–82; expansive, 79–83, 89; of photographs, 178; how to classify, 79–80; biography, 79; fiction, 79; history and travel, 79; juvenile books, 79; in the catalog, 78; on the shelves, 78–79.
Classification scheme, 34.
Classified reading (Lawrence), 32.
Cleveland summer school of library science, 155.
Cloth bindings, 102–103.
Club women, 169.
Club work, 169.
Clubs, 130; constitutions for, 168; organization of, 168; programs, 168; *see also* Library clubs, literary clubs, musical clubs.
Cole size card, 33, 94.
Collating books, 74, 100.
Commissions, free library, 149–150, 153.
Community and the library, 10, 12.
Complete sets, 66.
Conversation in the library, 121, 139.
Co-operation of teachers, 157–159, 160–162.
Copyright date on catalog cards, 94.
Covers for books, 75.
Crocker book support, 73.
Cross-reference cards, 97.

Cumulative index, 55.
Cutter's author table, 34, 90; expansive classification, 79, 83–89; rules for a dictionary catalog, 31
Date, copyright, on catalog cards, 94.
Date in charging system, 115, 116, 117; of publication, in accession book, 77; on catalog cards, 94; on order slip, 64.
Daters, 34, 115.
Dating slip, 115.
Dealers, *see* Book dealers.
Decimal classification, 79, 81–82.
Delivery room, 121.
Denison's labels, 34.
Denver public library handbook, 31.
Depository libraries, 108–109.
Dewey, or Decimal system of classification, 79, 81–82.
Dial (semi-monthly), 32.
Dictionaries, aid in reference work, 53.
Dictionary catalog, Cutter's rules for, 31; value of, 112; defined, 96.
Discarded books, 111.
Discounts, 63, 65–66–67.
Disjoined hand writing, 70–71.
Drexel institute library school, 155.
Duplicate catalog, 94.
Duplicates for school use, 149.
Dusting books, 74.
Duties of a librarian, 125–126, 144; of trustees, 18.
Editions, 63, 65–66–67.
Education through libraries, 13, 123–124, 133, 156, 160–162, 166, 170; *see also* Influence of the library.
Embossing stamps, 98.
Employés, appointment of, 18, 144; salaries of, 144; suspension of, 144.
English catalog, 30.

INDEX

Engravings, 129.
Entertainments, see Library entertainments.
Essentials of good binding (McNamee), 103, 105.
Exhibits, 170.
Expansive classification (Cutter), 79, 83-89.
Expenditures, 143.
Expiration of privileges, 119.
Faxon, F. W., Use of periodicals in reference work, 54-56.
Fiction, author-numbers for, 90; binding for, 103; cataloging, 95; cheap editions of, 66; classification of, 79; price per volume, 67; selecting, 41-42.
Figures, 71-72.
Finance committee, 142.
Fine slip, 119.
Fines, 116, 138.
Five thousand books, compiled for the Ladies' home journal, 31.
Fixtures for libraries, 26-27-28.
Fletcher, W. I., Libraries and recreation, 133; public libraries in America, 31.
Folios, binding for, 103-104.
Folsom, Channing, how the library can assist the school, 160-162.
Forfeiture of privileges, 138-139.
Free library commissions, 149-150.
Function of the library, 12, 15-16, 123-124, 133, 148.
Furniture for libraries, 27-28-29.
Gallery card, for painting and sculpture, 175.
Garfield, J. R., village library successfully managed, 135-136.
Gift book, 100; plates, 99-100.
Gifts, 130; acknowledgment of, 45, 77, 100, 145.
Glue, 105.

Guarantor, 118, 157.
Handwriting, brief rules for, 69-72.
Hasse, A. R., public decuments, 108-110.
Henderson, M. R., Librarian as host, 128-130.
Hiatt, C. W., Ideal library, 127.
Higgins' ink, 34, 69; photo mounter, 34.
Hints to small libraries (Plummer), 31.
History and travel, classification of, 79.
Home libraries, 166-167.
Hopkins, J. A., The trained librarian in a small library, 23-24.
How the library can assist the school (Folsom), 160-162.
Ideal library (Hiatt), 127.
Iles, George, Books for girls and women and their clubs, 32.
Imprint, for photographs, 178, 180; on catalog cards, 94.
Index, annual literary, 55; cumulative, 55; monthly cumulative book, 33; Poole's, 55; relative, 81; to borrowers, 119.
Indexes, their use taught, 159; to periodicals, 55.
Influence of the library, 12, 127; see also Education through libraries.
Information for borrowers, 137.
Ink, 34, 69; for photograph labels, 179; pads, 34, 98.
Inquiries, how to answer, 53.
Inventory taking, 111.
Joined hand writing, 70-71.
Juvenile books, binding for, 103; classification of, 79; periodicals, 58; price per volume, 67; selecting, 41, 66.
Kent, H. W., Rules for the care of photographs, 171, 180.
Labeling photographs, 178-179.

INDEX

Labels, for backs of books, 98-99, 101; gummed, 34; ink for, 34, 69; ink for photograph, 179; varnishing, 99, 101.
Law, library, 9.
Lawrence, I., Classified reading, 32.
Leather for bindings, 102, 104.
Lectures, 129, 149, 170.
Legislation, *see* Library legislation.
Librarian, advice to a, 125-126; and trustees, 18-19; annual report of, 145-146; appointment of, 20, 23, 25; as a host (Henderson), 128, 130; duties of a, 144; monthly report of, 145; qualifications of, 20-22, 122, 127, 154; the trained (Hopkins), 23-24.
Libraries and communities, 10, 12.
Libraries and clubs, 120, 168-169.
Libraries and education, 13, 123-124, 133.
Libraries and politics, 148.
Libraries and the public, 15, 121, 123-124.
Libraries and recreation (Fletcher), 133.
Libraries and schools, 13, 127, 157-159, 160-162; establishment and maintenance of, 147; function of, 12, 15-16, 123-124, 133, 148; management of, 15, 19, 127, 148.
Library advertising, *see* Advertising a library.
Library assistants, appointment of, 18.
Library associations, 152-153.
Library beginnings, 9-10.
Library board, *see* Trustees.
Library buildings and the community, 26.
Library buildings, architecture, 25-26; convenience, 26; decoration, 26; exterior, 25-26; fixtures, 26-27-28; furniture, 27-28-29; interior, 26-27; partitions, 27; requirements, 25; stairs, 27; windows, 26.
L. B. book support, 73.
L. B. pamphlet case, 106.
L. B. steel stacks, 37.
Library Bureau, relation to libraries (Meleney), 35-38; catalog of, 29, 31, 35-36; organization of, 35; publications of, 36, 38; cabinet works of, 37; card factory of, 37; consultation department, 35, 38; employment department, 35; supply department, 36.
Library clubs, 153.
Library entertainments, 128-130, 170.
Library journal (monthly), 32.
Library law, 9; essentials of a good, 151; outline of a good, 147; *see also* Library legislation.
Library league, 75.
Library league card, 120; reference list on, 150; *see also* Library law.
Library literature, 30-33, 36.
Library legislation (Patten), 147.
Library patrons, 131.
Library policy, 15-16, 127.
Library rooms, 25-26-27.
Library school rules, 30.
Library schools and training classes, aim and scope of, 154.
Library schools and training classes, list of, 155.
Library, the ideal, 127.
Light in libraries, 26.
List, of books for girls and women (Iles), 32, 168; of books needed in beginning work, 30-32; of periodicals for a small library, 61-62; of periodicals needed in beginning work, 32-33; of reference books, 46-52; of things needed

INDEX

in beginning work, 33-34; of things to be done to prepare books for shelves, 100-101.
Lists, of additions, 112; for reference, 112-113, 157, 161; for schools, 113, 157, 161; *see also* Bulletins.
Literary clubs and libraries (Moore), 168-169.
Literature, its use, 134.
Literature, library; *see* Library literature.
Literature (weekly), 32.
Loan department, 121, 133.
Local history, books on, 44.
Local history pamphlets, 106.
Los Angeles public library training class, 155.
Lost cards, 138.
McNamee, J. H. H., Essentials of good binding, 103-105.
Magazine binder, 58.
Magazine record, in blank book 60; on cards, 60.
Management of the library, 15, 19, 127, 148.
Manuscripts, *see* Ancient manuscripts.
Marking books, 98, 100.
Meeting of board of trustees, 140.
Meleney, G. B., Relation of the Library Bureau to libraries, 35-38.
Men's and Women's clubs, 168
Mending, *see* Repair.
Missing books, 111.
Monthly cumulative book index, 33.
Moore, E. L., Literary clubs and libraries, 168-169.
Morocco for bindings, 104.
Mucilage, 105.
Museums, 149, 170.
Musical clubs, 129, 168.
Musical entertainments, 129.
Nation (weekly) 32.
National educational association, 156.

Natural history collections, 170.
New books, 68.
New York state library commission, 150.
New York state library school, 155.
New York Times, 33.
Newspaper lists, 93, 113.
Newspapers, binding for, 103; files and racks for, 59; for the reading room, 57.
Non-depository libraries, 108.
Non-residents, 139.
Novel clubs, 168.
Officers of board of trustees, 18.
Open shelves, 15, 25, 121, 123-124, 163.
Order list, 100.
Order sheet, 64, 67.
Order slip, 63-64, 100.
Overdue books, 116, 138.
Overdue notice, 119.
Ownership, marks of, 98, 100.
Pages, cutting, 74, 100; entry in accession book, 77.
Painting card, author, 173; gallery, 175; school, 176; title, 174.
Pamphlet case, 106-107.
Pamphlets, cataloging, 106-107; classifying, 106-107; klips for, 107; local history, 106.
Paper, best quality for books, 63.
Paste, 34, 105.
Patten, F. C., Library legislation, 147.
Patrons, 131.
Penalties, 149.
Perforating stamp, 98.
Periodicals, binder for, 58-59; binding for, 104; circulation of, 59; cost, 59; for children, 58; indexes to, 55; list for a small library, 61-62; needed in beginning work, 32-33; record of, 60; use in reference work, 54-56.

INDEX

Photographs, 129; accessioning, 171-172; cataloging, 172-177; classifying, 178; labeling, 178-179; storage, 180; handling, 180.
Placards, see Signs.
Place of publication, in accession book, 77; on order slip, 64.
Planning library buildings (Soule), 25-29.
Plummer, M. W., Hints to small libraries, 31.
Pocket, see Book pocket.
Policy of the library, 15-16, 127.
Politics and libraries, 148.
Poole's index, 55.
Postal notice, 117.
Pratt institute library school, 155.
Preliminary work, 10.
Preparing books for the shelves, 98-101.
President of library board, 141.
Printed catalogs, 93, 113.
Printed rules, 137.
Privileges, expiration of, 119.
Privileges for children, 157; forfeiture of, 138-139; teachers, 138, 158.
Process, photograph, 172.
Professional books for teachers, 149.
Public, contact with the, 121; rules for the, 137-139.
Public documents, 44; care in a library, 109-110; check list, 109; collecting 44; congressional, 108-109-110; departmental, 108-109-110; how issued, 108; to whom issued, 108-109.
Public libraries (monthly), 32, 38.
Public libraries in America (Fletcher), 31.
Public library handbook, 31.
Publication, date of; see Date of publication.

Publication, place of; see Place of publication.
Publisher's name, in accession book, 77; on order slip, 64.
Publishers' trade list annual, 31.
Publishers' weekly, 32.
Punctuation, 94.
Purchase of books, see Buying books.
Qualifications of librarian, 20-22, 122, 127, 154.
Qualifications of trustees, 17.
Quorum of library board 140.
Rare bindings, collections, 170.
Rare books, 44-45.
Readers, 27.
Readers' guide to contemporary literature (Sonnenschein), 32.
Reading habits, 161-162.
Reading lists, see Reference lists.
Reading room, character of, 57; for children, 157, 163; newspapers for, 57; periodicals for, 58-60; rules for, 139; value of, 12-13.
Receptions, 170.
Recreation, 133.
Reference books, for a small library (Baker), 46-52; for schools, 149, 160, 165; how indicated, 138; selecting, 39.
Reference catalog of current literature, 31.
Reference department, 139.
Reference list on library legislation, 150.
Reference lists, for schools, 113, 157, 161; on cards, 54; special subject, 112.
Reference work, for children, 159, 160, 163, 165; suggestions, 53; use of dictionaries, 53; use of periodicals, 54-56.
Register of borrowers, see Borrowers.
Regulations, see Rules for the public.

INDEX

Relation of the Library Bureau to libraries (Meleney), 35-38.
Relative index, 81.
Remainder libraries, 108, 109.
Renewal of books, 116, 138.
Repair, 105.
Report, annual, 146; of librarian, 145; of trustees, 143.
Request blanks, 45.
Responsibility of borrowers, 118, 138, 157.
Review of reviews, 55.
Rooms, library, 25-26-27.
Rubber stamps, 34, 98.
Rules, accession-book, 30, 77; card catalog, 30, 94-96; for an author and title catalog, condensed, 31; for a dictionary catalog, 31, 96; for binding, 105; for care of books, 75; for government of trustees and employes, 140-145; for handwriting, 69-72; for the care of photographs (Kent), 171-180. for the public, 15, 121, 137-139; library school, 30; shelf list, 30, 91-92; for planning library buildings (Soule), 25-29.
Sargent's reading for the young, 55.
School card for painting and sculpture, 175-176.
School libraries, 149, 160, 164-165.
Schoolroom libraries, *see* School libraries.
Schools and libraries, 13, 127, 157-159, 160-162, 164.
Schools, reference books for, 149, 160, 165.
Schools, reference lists for, 113, 157, 161.
Second-hand books, 66, 68.
Secretary of library board, 141.
Selection of books, extra copies, 42, 44; fiction, 41-42; for children, 41; for reference, 39; history, travel, literature, 41; local history, 44; natural science, 43; price, 40, 41; proportion in each department, 43; public documents, 44; rare books, 44, 45; request blanks, 45, 65; suggestions, 39; with reference to the community, 40, 43, 68; *see also* Buying books.
Series, 66.
Shelf-list cards, 34, 92.
Shelf-list rules, 30, 91-92.
Shelf-list sheets, 34, 91.
Shelves, for folios and quartos, 27; form, 27; height, 26; size, 27.
Signs, 57, 121.
Size card, 33.
Size letter, 94.
Size notation for photographs, 172, 178, 180.
Size of board of trustees, 17.
Societies, *see* Clubs.
Sonnenschein, W. S., Best books, 31; readers' guide to contemporaneous literature, 32.
Soule, C. C., Rules for planning library buildings, 25, 29; trustees, 17, 19.
Special libraries, 109.
Specialists, 129.
Stafford's ink, 69.
Stacks, 28, 37.
Stamp, embossing, 98; perforating, 98; rubber, 34, 98; rubber, for labeling photographs, 179.
Stamping books, 98, 100.
State library commissions, 149-150, 153.
State library associations, 153.
Storage of photographs, 180.
Study clubs, 168.
Style card for architecture, 177.
Subject card, illustration, 96.
Subject headings, 32, 95-97.
Subject-list, 95.
Supplementary reading for schools, 149, 160.
Supplies, 29-30-34, 36.

INDEX

Supports, 73.
Tables, 27.
Tax levy for libraries, 147–148.
Teachers' cards, 158.
Teachers, coöperation of, 157–159–160–162.
Teachers' privileges, 138, 158.
Teachers, professional books for, 149.
Things needed in beginning work, 33–34.
Time limit for retaining books, 138.
Title, in accession book, 77; in catalog, 94; on order slip, 64; on shelf-list, 84.
Title card, illustration, 95; for architecture, 176; for painting and sculpture, 174–175.
Title-lists, 95, 113.
Tools, 30–34.
Tools, books as useful, 134.
Trained librarian in a small library (Hopkins), 23–24.
Training classes, 154–155.
Transfer of accounts, 138.
Traveling libraries, 150, 169.
Tray, for book cards, 115; for catalog cards, 97.
Trustees, appointment of, 148; committees, 18, 142; duties, 18; meeting of board of, 140; officers, 18, 141; qualifications, 17; relations with the librarian, 18–19; reports, 143; size of board, 17; term of office 17, 148.
Two-book system, 117.
Type, size of, 63.
U. S. documents, *see* Public documents.
University of Illinois state library school, 155.
Varnish for labels, 99.
Vertical hand, 69.
Village library successfully managed (Garfield), 135–136.
Volume entry in accession book, 76.
Wisconsin summer school of library science, 155.
Women on library board, 136.
Women's clubs, 168–169.
Work-number, *see* Book-number.
World's library congress papers, 32.
Writing, *see* Handwriting.
Young ladies' clubs, 168.
Young men's clubs, 168.
Young people, reading for; *see* Juvenile books.

www.ingramcontent.com/pod-product-compliance
Lightning Source LLC
Chambersburg PA
CBHW020243170426
43202CB00008B/204